PARNASSUS EN ROUTE

Parnassus en Route

AN ANTHOLOGY OF POEMS ABOUT PLACES,
NOT PEOPLE, ON THE EUROPEAN CONTINENT

COMPILED BY
KENNETH HORAN

*As the Spanish proverb says, "He who would
bring home the wealth of the Indies, must carry
the wealth of the Indies with him."*

Granger Index Reprint Series

BOOKS FOR LIBRARIES PRESS
FREEPORT, NEW YORK

First Published 1929
Reprinted 1972

INTERNATIONAL STANDARD BOOK NUMBER:
0-8369-6332-6

LIBRARY OF CONGRESS CATALOG CARD NUMBER:
70-38600

PRINTED IN THE UNITED STATES OF AMERICA
BY
NEW WORLD BOOK MANUFACTURING CO., INC.
HALLANDALE, FLORIDA 33009

TO MY FRIEND

M. B. H.

WITH MORE THAN CAN EVER BE SAID

INTRODUCTION

The lady whose joy in life is travel, was packing her trunk. It consisted in a layer of books, a layer of finery, another layer of books, and so on, till the bulging sides refused to meet. The thought of the various expressmen in all the lands of the world, their various sagging shoulders and their various aching backs, as they piloted this ton of knowledge and adornment over the face of the earth oppressed me. The lady whose joy in life is travel seemed unoppressed.

"Like moving a mountain," she carolled blithely, pushing the "Lays of Ancient Rome" between a pair of silver slippers.

"A mountain? Parnassus," I answered gloomily. "Parnassus en route."

"Well, why can't something be done about it?" she responded with her customary briskness—she is quick to be diverted from the homely task of the day to enter into abstruse problems. "Why don't you collect the poems that have to do with all the places I must see before I die, so that when I look at the Acropolis by moonlight I shan't have to gnash my teeth to remember who said what about it. . . . I can't see places without thinking of all the others who have seen them! I can't feel the beauty of a country without thinking of all the others who have felt its beauty! Beauty," with a jab at a reluctant hat, wedged between Lord Byron and Edna Millay, "must be shared to be enjoyed. What other eyes have seen, mine love to view."

And that, by the way, is the charm of the lady whose joy in life is travel. She has in all things, even in the passing of time, a joie de vivre.

It is true, as she says, that the experience of beauty shared is equaled only by the experience of sorrow shared, and in junketing from land to land, the past and present meet in both. Madame de Staël has said that "travelling is the saddest of all pleasures." We all know that, but we are ready, none the less, to leave the happy valley of home for new scenes. There is between travellers a kind of free-masonry. To have visited the same places is a bond of sympathy between those who have no other point of contact. A vague interest surrounds the man whom we have met in a foreign land, and even reserved and silent people become talkative when the conversation turns on countries they have seen. The Poets are the best travelling companions of all, for they discern so many things that are invisible to common eyes.

"Language," says Talleyrand, "is a medium for concealing thought." Not so with poetry. It is the medium for expressing emotion of one kind or another. And the places where these emotions have been experienced, are the places we seek. Old things become alive when touched with an appreciation of their beauty or their significance, and involuntarily we long for the companionship of those who have so touched them.

"If," continued the lady whose joy in life is travel, "if you would select some of the poems from all these books that have to do with places I must see before I die, my trunk would weigh less and my mind would weigh more."

For her sake and for mine, and for the sake of all the anxious people in the world who also feel they must see many places before they die, this collection has been made. It strives to present the best that has been written of each famous spot on the well travelled continent. If some of

your favorites or mine have been left out, so in any jour-
ney there are places which, however beautiful and signifi-
cant, must be, for want of time or space, regretfully
passed by.

K. H.

CONTENTS

[xi]

IRELAND

SCOTLAND

WALES

BELGIUM

[xv]

[xvii]

[xviii]

[xix]

HOMEWARD BOUND

OUTWARD BOUND

SEA-FEVER

I must go down to the seas again, to the lonely sea and the
    sky,
And all I ask is a tall ship and a star to steer her by,
And the wheel's kick and the wind's song and the white sail's
    shaking,
And a grey mist on the sea's face and a grey dawn breaking.

I must go down to the seas again, for the call of the running
    tide
Is a wild call and a clear call that may not be denied;
And all I ask is a windy day with the white clouds flying,
And the flung spray and the blown spume, and the sea-gulls
    crying.

I must go down to the seas again to the vagrant gypsy life,
To the gull's way and the whale's way where the wind's
    like a whetted knife;
And all I ask is a merry yarn from a laughing fellow-rover,
And quiet sleep and a sweet dream when the long trick's
    over.

John Masefield

ON THE SEA

It keeps eternal whisperings around
Desolate shores, and with its mighty swell
Gluts twice ten thousand Caverns, till the spell
Of Hecate leaves them their old shadowy sound.
Often 'tis in such gentle temper found,
That scarcely will the very smallest shell
Be moved for days from whence it sometime fell
When last the winds of Heaven were unbound.
Oh ye! who have your eye-balls vexed and tired,
Feast them upon the wideness of the Sea;
Oh ye! whose ears are dinned with uproar rude,
Or fed too much with cloying melody,—
Sit ye near some old cavern's mouth, and brood
Until ye start, as if the sea-nymphs quired!

John Keats

England

*John Bull's island, "perfidious Albion,"
home of the ancient Briton, inhabited by the
descendants of Hengist and Horsa, of Angle
and Saxon, of Frisian and Dane, of Norman
and Celt; where Arthur kept tryst with his
knights of the Round Table; the land of the
Druids and of Alfred the Great; renowned
for Chaucer and Spenser and Shakespeare and
Shelley and Keats, and for the gloomy dean of
St. Paul's who thunders forth dire portents
for the Empire; land of good brown ale, and
of roast mutton and tipsy pudding; of Bond
Street and St. James; famous for Westmin-
ster Abbey and for the horsemanship of Albert
Edward; "Merrie England" in fact, for in
spite of a world war Tommy Atkins still
carries on.*

THE WHITE CLIFFS

Woden made the red cliffs, the red walls of England.
  Round, the South of Devonshire, they burn against the
      blue.
Green is the water there; and, clear as liquid sunlight,
  Blue-green as mackerel, the bays that Raleigh knew.

Thor made the black cliffs, the battlements of England,
  Climbing to Tintagel where the white gulls wheel.
Cold are the caverns there, and sullen as a cannon-mouth,
  Booming back the grey swell that gleams like steel.

Balder made the white cliffs, the white shield of England
  (Crowned with thyme and violet where Sussex wheat-ears
      fly).
White as the White Ensign are the bouldered heights of
      Dover,
  Beautiful the scutcheon that they bare against the sky.

So the world shall sing of them—the white cliffs of England,
  White, the glory of her sails, the banner of her pride.
One and all,—their seamen met and broke the dread Armada.
  Only white may show the world the shield for which they
      died.

                                        Alfred Noyes

ENGLAND

No lovelier hills than thine have laid
  My tired thoughts to rest:
No peace of lovelier valleys made
  Like peace within my breast.

Thine are the woods whereto my soul,
  Out of the noontide beam,
Flees for a refuge green and cool
  And tranquil as a dream.

Thy breaking seas like trumpets peal;
  Thy clouds—how oft have I
Watched their bright towers of silence steal
  Into infinity!

My heart within me faints to roam
  In thought even far from thee:
Thine be the grave whereto I come,
  And thine my darkness be.

Walter de la Mare

HOME-THOUGHTS, FROM ABROAD

O, to be in England
Now that April's there,
And whoever wakes in England
Sees, some morning, unaware,
That the lowest boughs and the brushwood sheaf
Round the elm-tree bole are in tiny leaf,
While the chaffinch sings on the orchard bough
In England—now!

And after April, when May follows,
And the whitethroat builds, and all the swallows!
Hark, where my blossom'd pear-tree in the hedge
Leans to the field and scatters on the clover
Blossoms and dewdrops—at the bent spray's edge—
That's the wise thrush; he sings each song twice over,
Lest you should think he never could recapture
The first fine careless rapture!
And though the fields look rough with hoary dew,
All will be gay when noontide wakes anew
The buttercups, the little children's dower
—Far brighter than this gaudy melon-flower!

Robert Browning

DOVER BEACH

The sea is calm to-night.
The tide is full, the moon lies fair
Upon the straits;—on the French coast the light
Gleams and is gone; the cliffs of England stand,
Glimmering and vast, out in the tranquil bay.
Come to the window, sweet is the night-air!
Only, from the long line of spray
Where the sea meets the moon-blanched land,
Listen! you hear the grating roar
Of pebbles which the waves draw back, and fling,
At their return, up the high strand,
Begin, and cease, and then again begin,
With tremulous cadence slow, and bring
The eternal note of sadness in.

Sophocles long ago
Heard it on the Ægæan, and it brought
Into his mind the turbid ebb and flow
Of human misery; we
Find also in the sound a thought,
Hearing it by this distant northern sea.

The sea of faith
Was once, too, at the full, and round earth's shore
Lay like the folds of a bright girdle furled.
But now I only hear
Its melancholy, long, withdrawing roar,
Retreating, to the breath
Of the night-wind, down the vast edges drear
And naked shingles of the world.

Ah, love, let us be true
To one another! for the world, which seems
To lie before us like a land of dreams,
So various, so beautiful, so new,
Hath really neither joy, nor love, nor light,
Nor certitude, nor peace, nor help for pain;
And we are here as on a darkling plain
Swept with confused alarms of struggle and flight,
Where ignorant armies clash by night.

Matthew Arnold

ENGLAND, MY ENGLAND

What have I done for you,
    England, my England?
What is there I would not do,
    England, my own?
With your glorious eyes austere,
As the Lord were walking near,
Whispering terrible things and dear
    As the Song on your bugles blown,
        England—
    Round the world on your bugles blown!

Where shall the watchful sun,
    England, my England,
Match the master-work you've done,
    England, my own?
When shall he rejoice agen
Such a breed of mighty men
As come forward, one to ten,
    To the Song on your bugles blown,
        England—
    Down the years on your bugles blown?

Ever the faith endures,
    England, my England:—
'Take and break us: we are yours,
    England, my own!
Life is good, and joy runs high
Between English earth and sky:
Death is death; but we shall die
    To the Song on your bugles blown,
        England—
    To the stars on your bugles blown!'

They call you proud and hard,
  England, my England:
You with worlds to watch and ward,
  England, my own!
You whose mail'd hand keeps the keys
Of such teeming destinies,
You could know nor dread nor ease
  Were the Song on your bugles blown,
    England—
  Round the Pit on your bugles blown!

Mother of Ships whose might,
  England, my England,
Is the fierce old Sea's delight,
  England, my own,
Chosen daughter of the Lord,
Spouse-in-Chief of the ancient Sword,
There's the menace of the Word
  In the Song on your bugles blown,
    England—
  Out of heaven on your bugles blown!

William Ernest Henley

NOVEMBER BLUE

The golden tint of the electric lights seems to give a complementary colour to the air in the early evening.
Essay on London.

O heavenly colour, London town
    Has blurred it from her skies;
And, hooded in an earthly brown,
    Unheaven'd the city lies.
No longer standard-like this hue
    Above the broad road flies;
Nor does the narrow street the blue
    Wear, slender pennon-wise.

But when the gold and silver lamps
    Colour the London dew,
And, misted by the winter damps,
    The shops shine bright anew—
Blue comes to earth, it walks the street,
    It dyes the wide air through;
A mimic sky about their feet,
    The throng go crowned with blue.

Alice Meynell

LONDON BEAUTIFUL

London, I heard one say, no more is fair,
London whose loveliness is everywhere,
London so beautiful at morning light
One half forgets how fair she is at night,
London as beautiful at set of sun
As though her beauty had but just begun;
London, that mighty sob, that splendid tear,
That jewel hanging in the great world's ear.
Strange queen of all this grim romantic stone,
Paris, say some, shall push you from your throne,
And all the tumbled beauty of your dreams
Submit to map and measure, straight cold schemes
Which for the loveliness that comes by chance
Shall substitute the conscious streets of France,
A beauty made for beauty that has grown,
An alien beauty, London, for your own.

Oh, wistful eyes so full of mist and tears,
Long be it ere your haunted vision clears,
Long ere the blood of your great heart shall flow
Through inexpressive avenue and row;
Straight-stepping, prim, the once adventurous stream,
Its spirit gone, it loiters not to dream,
All straight and pretty, trees on either side,
For London's beauty London beautified.
Ah! of your beauty change no single grace,
My London with your sad mysterious face.

                              Richard Le Gallienne

ROMANCES

As I came down the Highgate Hill,
The Highgate Hill, the Highgate Hill,
As I came down the Highgate Hill,
I met the sun's bravado,
And saw below me, fold on fold,
Grey to pearl and pearl to gold
This London like a land of old,
The land of Eldorado.

Henry Bashford

LONDON IN "DON JUAN"

(Canto X, Stanza 82)

A mighty mass of brick, and smoke, and shipping,
Dirty and dusty, but as wide as eye
Could reach, with here and there a sail just skipping
In sight, then lost amidst the forestry
Of masts; a wilderness of steeples peeping
On tiptoe through their sea-coal canopy,
A huge, dun cupola, like a foolscap crown
On a fool's head—and there is London town!

Lord Byron

IN HONOUR OF THE CITY OF LONDON

London, thou art of townes *A per se*.
  Soveraign of cities, seemliest in sight,
Of high renoun, riches and royaltie;
  Of lordis, barons, and many a goodly knyght;
  Of most delectable lusty ladies bright;
Of famous prelatis, in habitis clericall;
  Of merchauntis full of substaunce and of myght:
London, thou art the flour of Cities all.

Gladdith anon, thou lusty Troy novaunt,
  Citie that some tyme cleped was New Troy;
In all the erth, imperiall as thou stant,
  Pryncesse of townes, of pleasure and of joy,
  A richer restith under no Christen roy;
For manly power, with craftis naturall,
  Fourmeth none fairer sith the flode of Noy:
London, thou art the flour of Cities all.

Gemme of all joy, jasper of jocunditie,
  Most myghty carbuncle of vertue and valour;
Strong Troy in vigour and in strenuytie;
  Of royall cities rose and geraflour;
  Empress of townes, exalt in honour;
In beawtie beryng the crone imperiall;
  Swete paradise precelling in pleasure;
London, thou art the flour of Cities all.

Above all ryvers thy Ryver hath renowne,
  Whose beryall stremys, pleasant and preclare,
Under thy lusty wallys renneth down,
  Where many a swan doth swymme with wyngis fair;

[16]

Where many a barge doth saile and row with are;
Where many a ship doth rest with top-royall.
O, towne of townes! patrone and not compare,
London, thou art the flour of Cities all.

Upon thy lusty Brigge of pylers white
  Been merchauntis full royall to behold;
Upon thy stretis goeth many a semely knyght
  In velvet gownes and in cheynes of gold.
  By Julyus Cesar thy Tour founded of old
May be the hous of Mars victoryall,
  Whose artillary with tonge may not be told:
London, thou art the flour of Cities all.

Strong be thy wallis that about thee standis;
  Wise be the people that within thee dwellis;
Fresh is thy ryver with his lusty strandis;
  Bl:+h be thy chirches, wele sownyng be thy bellis;
  Rich be thy merchauntis in substaunce that excellis;
Fair be their wives, right lovesom, white and small;
  Clere be thy virgyns, lusty under kellis:
London, thou art the flour of Cities all.

Thy famous Maire, by pryncely governaunce,
  With sword of justice thee ruleth prudently.
No Lord of Parys, Venyce, or Floraunce
  In dignitye or honour goeth to hym nigh.
  He is exampler, loode-ster, and guye;
Principall patrone and rose orygynalle,
  Above all Maires as maister most worthy:
London, thou art the flour of Cities all.

                                    William Dunbar

[17]

LONDON

London, my beautiful,
it is not the sunset
nor the pale green sky
shimmering through the curtain
of the silver birch,
nor the quietness;
it is not the hopping
of birds
upon the lawn,
nor the darkness
stealing over all things
that moves me.

But as the moon creeps slowly
over the tree-tops
among the stars,
I think of her
and the glow her passing
sheds on men.

London, my beautiful,
I will climb
into the branches
to the moonlit tree-tops,
that my blood may be cooled
by the wind.

F. S. Flint

A BALLAD OF LONDON

Ah, London! London! our delight,
Great flower that opens but at night,
Great City of the midnight sun,
Whose day begins when day is done.

Lamp after lamp against the sky
Opens a sudden beaming eye,
Leaping alight on either hand,
The iron lilies of the Strand.

Like dragonflies, the hansoms hover,
With jeweled eyes, to catch the lover;
The streets are full of lights and loves,
Soft gowns, and flutter of soiled doves.

The human moths about the light
Dash and cling close in dazed delight,
And burn and laugh, the world and wife,
For this is London, this is life!

Upon thy petals butterflies,
But at thy root, some say, there lies,
A world of weeping trodden things,
Poor worms that have not eyes nor wings.

From out corruption of their woe
Springs this bright flower that charms us so,
Men die and rot deep out of sight
To keep this jungle-flower bright.

Paris and London, World-Flowers twain
Wherewith the World-Tree blooms again,

Since Time hath gathered Babylon,
And withered Rome still withers on.

Sidon and Tyre were such as ye,
How bright they shone upon the tree!
But Time hath gathered, both are gone,
And no man sails to Babylon.

Richard Le Gallienne

IMPRESSION DU MATIN

The Thames nocturne of blue and gold
  Changed to a harmony in grey;
  A barge with ochre-coloured hay
Dropt from the wharf: and chill and cold

The yellow fog came creeping down
  The bridges, till the houses' walls
  Seemed changed to shadows, and St. Paul's
Loomed like a bubble o'er the town.

Then suddenly arose the clang
  Of waking life; the streets were stirred
  With country waggons; and a bird
Flew to the glistening roofs and sang.

But one pale woman all alone,
  The daylight kissing her wan hair,
  Loitered beneath the gas lamps' flare,
With lips of flame and heart of stone.

Oscar Wilde

FLEET STREET

I never see the newsboys run
  Amid the whirling street,
  With swift untiring feet,
To cry the latest venture done,
But I expect one day to hear
  Them cry the crack of doom
  And risings from the tomb,
With great Archangel Michael near;
And see them running from the Fleet
  As messengers of God,
  With Heaven's tidings shod
About their brave unwearied feet.

Shane Leslie

IN WESTMINSTER ABBEY

*"The Southern Transept, hardly known
by any other name but Poets' Corner."*
                                    Dean Stanley

Tread softly here; the sacredest of tombs
Are those that hold your Poets.   Kings and queens
Are facile accidents of Time and Chance.
Chance sets them on the heights, they climb not there!
But he who from the darkling mass of men
Is on the wing of heavenly thought upborne
To finer ether, and becomes a voice
For all the voiceless, God anointed him:
His name shall be a star, his grave a shrine.

Tread softly here, in silent reverence tread.
Beneath those marble cenotaphs and urns
Lies richer dust than ever nature hid
Packed in the mountain's adamantine heart,
Or slyly wrapped in unsuspected sand—
The dross men toil for, and oft stain the soul.
How vain and all ignoble seems that greed
To him who stands in this dim claustral air
With these most sacred ashes at his feet!
This dust was Chaucer, Spenser, Dryden this—
The spark that once illumed it lingers still.
O ever hallowed spot of English earth!
If the unleashed and happy spirit of man
Have option to revisit our dull globe,
What august Shades at midnight here convene
In the miraculous sessions of the moon,
When the great pulse of London faintly throbs,
And one by one the constellations pale!

                                    Thomas Bailey Aldrich

THE LONDON BOBBY

The finest thing in London is the Bobby;
Benignant information is his hobby.
Don't be autobiographic
While he's regulating traffic,
But when less pronounced congestion
Gives him leisure, put your question,
And without the slightest fuss
He will designate the bus
That will take you out to Stratford,
Brixton, Clapham Junction, Catford,
Hendon, Plaistow, Horselydown,
Cricklewood,—or any town
Street or district that you're bound for;
'Tis a thing that he's renowned for.
Who so amiably efficient,
Who so helpfully omniscient,
Who so humorously gentle
So indulgently parental?
When you're stupefied and silly
In the rush of Piccadilly,
When you're feeling lost and sobby,—
Yes, the finest thing in London is the Bobby!

Oh, of course you'll see the Tower
Where when knighthood was in flower
They decapitated traitors,
Nobles, queens and legislators;
Then they'll show you old St. Paul's,
Crumbling bits of Roman walls,
Galleries of wondrous treasures,
Public parks for simple pleasures,

Palaces remotely dated,
Vaulted chambers consecrated
By Elizabeth the Spinster,
And the Abbey of Westminster
And the House of Commons lobby;—
But the finest thing in London is the Bobby!

Arthur Guiterman

ST. JAMES'S STREET

St. James's Street, of classic fame,
   For Fashion still is seen there:
St. James's Street? I know the name,
   I almost think I've been there!
Why, that's where Sacharissa sighed
   When Waller read his ditty;
Where Byron lived, and Gibbon died,
   And Alvanley was witty.

A famous Street! To yonder Park
   Young Churchill stole in class-time;
Come, gaze on fifty men of mark,
   And then recall the past time.
The *plats* at White's, the play at Crock's,
   The bumpers to Miss Gunning;
The *bonhomie* of Charley Fox,
   And Selwyn's ghastly funning.

The dear old Street of clubs and cribs,
   As north and south it stretches,
Still seems to smack of Rolliad squibs,
   And Gillray's fiercer sketches;
The quaint old dress, the grand old style,
   The *mots,* the racy stories;
The wine, the dice, the wit, the bile —
   The hate of Whigs and Tories.

At dusk, when I am strolling there,
   Dim forms will rise around me;
Lepel flits past me in her chair,
   And Congreve's airs astound me!

And once Nell Gwynne, a frail young Sprite,
   Looked kindly when I met her;
I shook my head, perhaps,—but quite
   Forgot to quite forget her.

The Street is still a lively tomb
   For rich, and gay, and clever;
The crops of dandies bud and bloom,
   And die as fast as ever.
Now gilded youth loves cutty pipes,
   And slang that's rather scaring;
It can't approach its prototypes
   In taste, or tone, or bearing.

In Brummell's day of buckle shoes,
   Lawn cravats, and roll collars,
They'd fight, and woo, and bet—and lose,
   Like gentlemen and scholars:
I'm glad young men should go the pace,
   I half forgive Old Rapid!
These louts disgrace their name and race—
   So vicious and so vapid!

Worse times may come. *Bon ton,* indeed,
   Will then be quite forgotten,
And all we much revere will speed
   From ripe to worse than rotten:
Let grass then sprout between yon stones,
   And owls then roost at Boodle's,
For Echo will hurl back the tones
   Of screaming Yankee Doodles.

I love the haunts of old Cockaigne,
　　Where wit and wealth were squandered;
The halls that tell of hoop and train,
　　Where grace and rank have wandered;
Those halls where ladies fair and leal
　　First ventured to adore me!
Something of that old love I feel
　　For this old Street before me.

Frederick Locker-Lampson

AT THE BRITISH MUSEUM

I turn the page and read:
"I dream of silent verses where the rhyme
Glides noiseless as an oar."
The heavy musty air, the black desks,
The bent heads and the rustling noises
In the great dome
Vanish . . .
And
The sun hangs in the cobalt-blue sky,
The boat drifts over the lake shallows,
The fishes skim like umber shades through the undulating
      weeds,
The oleanders drop their rosy petals on the lawns,
And the swallows dive and swirl and whistle
About the cleft battlements of Can Grande's castle. . . .

Richard Aldington

SONNET

Composed Upon Westminster Bridge,
September 3, 1802

Earth has not anything to show more fair:
Dull would he be of soul who could pass by
A sight so touching in its majesty:
This City now doth, like a garment, wear
The beauty of the morning; silent, bare,
Ships, towers, domes, theaters, and temples lie
Open unto the fields, and to the sky;
All bright and glittering in the smokeless air.
Never did sun more beautifully steep
In his first splendor, valley, rock, or hill;
Ne'er saw I, never felt, a calm so deep!
The river glideth at his own sweet will:
Dear God! the very houses seem asleep;
And all that mighty heart is lying still!

William Wordsworth

GUILIELMUS REX

The folk who lived in Shakespeare's day
And saw that gentle figure pass
By London Bridge, his frequent way—
They little knew what man he was.

The pointed beard, the courteous mien,
The equal port to high and low,
All this they saw or might have seen—
But not the light behind the brow!

The doublet's modest gray or brown,
The slender sword-hilt's plain device,
What sign had these for prince or clown?
Few turned, or none, to scan them twice.

Yet 'twas the king of England's kings!
The rest with all their pomps and trains
Are mouldered, half-remembered things—
'Tis he alone that lives and reigns!

Thomas Bailey Aldrich

THE DAFFODILS OF OLD SAINT PAUL'S

Call delicately through the town;
   "Let April have its will;
Oh, run; oh, run to Old Saint Paul's
   And buy a daffodil!

A rosy vicar saw their kind
   Three hundred years ago,
And thrust them on a Devon shelf
   Where they are still in blow.

Could Herrick come to Old Saint Paul's
   With our tall flowers so gay,
He would not have the heart indeed
   To tear himself away.

The hawker sets them on the curb
   Like candles thereabout;
Oh, buy your one; oh, buy your two,
   Before they splutter out!"

Lizette Woodworth Reese

ST. JOHN'S, CAMBRIDGE

I stand beneath the tree, whose branches shade
Thy western window, Chapel of St. John!
And hear its leaves repeat their benison
On him, whose hand thy stones memorial laid;
Then I remember one of whom was said
In the world's darkest hour, "Behold thy son!"
And see him living still, and wandering on
And waiting for the advent long delayed.
Not only tongues of the apostles teach
Lessons of love and light, but these expanding
And sheltering boughs with all their leaves implore,
And say in language clear as human speech,
"The peace of God, that passeth understanding,
Be and abide with you forevermore."

Henry Wadsworth Longfellow

IMPRESSION DE NUIT: LONDON

See what a mass of gems the city wears
Upon her broad live bosom! row on row,
Rubies and emeralds and amethysts glow.
See that huge circle, like a necklace stares
With thousand of bold eyes to heaven, and dares
The golden stars to dim the lamps below,
And in the mirror of the mire I know
The moon has left her image unawares.

That's the great town at night; I see her breasts,
Prick'ed out with lamps they stand like huge black towers.
I think they move! I hear her panting breath.
And that's her head where the tiara rests.
And in her brain, through lanes as dark as death,
Men creep like thoughts. . . . The lamps are like pale
    flowers.

Lord Alfred Douglas

LINES COMPOSED A FEW MILES ABOVE
TINTERN ABBEY

Five years have past; five summers, with the length
Of five long winters! and again I hear
These waters, rolling from their mountain-springs
With a sweet inland murmur.—Once again
Do I behold these steep and lofty cliffs,
That on a wild secluded scene impress
Thoughts of more deep seclusion; and connect
The landscape with the quiet of the sky.
The day is come when I again repose
Here, under this dark sycamore, and view
These plots of cottage-ground, these orchard-tufts,
Which at this season, with their unripe fruits,
Are clad in one green hue, and lose themselves
Among the woods and copses, nor disturb
The wild green landscape. Once again I see
These hedge-rows, hardly hedge-rows, little lines
Of sportive wood run wild: these pastoral farms,
Green to the very door; and wreaths of smoke
Sent up, in silence, from among the trees!
With some uncertain notice, as might seem
Of vagrant dwellers in the houseless woods,
Or of some Hermit's cave, where by his fire
The Hermit sits alone.

William Wordsworth

CORNISH WIND

There is a wind in Cornwall that I know
From any other wind, because it smells
Of the warm honey breath of heather-bells
And of the sea's salt; and these meet and flow
With such sweet savour in such sharpness met
That the astonished sense in ecstasy
Tastes the ripe earth and the unvintaged sea.
Wind out of Cornwall, wind, if I forget:
Not in the tunnelled streets where scarce men breathe
The air they live by, but whatever seas
Blossom in foam, wherever merchant bees
Volubly traffic upon any heath:
If I forget, shame me! or if I find
A wind in England like my Cornish wind.

Arthur Symons

A GHOST OUT OF STRATFORD

For all the crowd that packed the house to-night,
   Marked you the vacant seat none came to claim, . . .
The fourth row from the front, and to the right? . . .
   Vacant, I call it now. . . . But I could name
A thing that happened when the lights were off,
   Of one who walked in buckles down the aisle,
Wearing a great hat that he scorned to doff,
   And richly kerchiefed, wrist and neck in style.

Once in the play—I swear it—once I heard,
   Along the tumult of our loud applause,
A sly and ghostly chuckle at a word
   That Falstaff mouthed with those outrageous jaws . . .
I think he liked the play . . . and stayed, no doubt,
   Long after us, and lingered going out.

David Morton

AN ELEGY WRITTEN IN A COUNTRY CHURCHYARD

(STOKE POGES)

First Nine Stanzas

The curfew tolls the knell of parting day,
  The lowing herd wind slowly o'er the lea,
The ploughman homeward plods his weary way,
  And leaves the world to darkness and to me.

Now fades the glimmering landscape on the sight,
  And all the air a solemn stillness holds,
Save where the beetle wheels his droning flight,
  And drowsy tinklings lull the distant folds.

Save that from yonder ivy-mantled tow'r,
  The moping owl does to the moon complain
Of such as, wand'ring near her secret bow'r,
  Molest her ancient solitary reign.

Beneath those rugged elms, that yew-tree's shade,
  Where heaves the turf in many a mould'ring heap
Each in his narrow cell forever laid,
  The rude forefathers of the hamlet sleep.

The breezy call of incense-breathing morn,
  The swallow twitt'ring from the straw-built shed
The cock's shrill clarion, or the echoing horn,
  No more shall rouse them from their lowly bed.

For them no more the blazing hearth shall burn,
  Or busy housewife ply her evening care;
No children run to lisp their sire's return,
  Or climb his knees the envied kiss to share.

[38]

Oft did the harvest to their sickle yield,
    Their furrow oft the stubborn glebe, has broke:
How jocund did they drive their team afield!
    How bow'd the woods beneath their sturdy stroke!

Let not Ambition mock their useful toil,
    Their homely joys, and destiny obscure;
Nor Grandeur hear with a disdainful smile
    The short and simple annals of the poor.

The boast of heraldry, the pomp of pow'r,
    And all that beauty, all that wealth e'er gave,
Await alike th' inevitable hour,
    The paths of glory lead but to the grave.

                                        Thomas Gray

THE SOUTH COUNTRY

When I am living in the Midlands
  That are sodden and unkind,
I light my lamp in the evening:
  My work is left behind;
And the great hills of the South Country
  Come back into my mind.

The great hills of the South Country
  They stand along the sea;
And it's there walking in the high woods
  That I could wish to be,
And the men that were boys when I was a boy
  Walking along with me.

The men that live in North England
  I saw them for a day:
Their hearts are set upon the waste fells,
  Their skies are fast and grey;
From their castle-walls a man may see
  The mountains far away.

The men that live in West England
  They see the Severn strong,
A-rolling on rough water brown
  Light aspen leaves along.
They have the secret of the Rocks,
  And the oldest kind of song.

But the men that live in the South Country
  Are the kindest and most wise,
They get their laughter from the loud surf,
  And the faith in their happy eyes

Comes surely from our Sister the Spring
    When over the sea she flies;
The violets suddenly bloom at her feet,
    She blesses us with surprise.

I never get between the pines
    But I smell the Sussex air;
Nor I never come on a belt of sand
    But my home is there.
And along the sky the line of the Downs
    So noble and so bare.

A lost thing could I never find,
    Nor a broken thing mend:
And I fear I shall be all alone
    When I get towards the end.
Who will there be to comfort me
    Or who will be my friend?

I will gather and carefully make my friends
    Of the men of the Sussex Weald;
They watch the stars from silent folds,
    They stiffly plough the field.
By them and the God of the South Country
    My poor soul shall be healed.

If I ever become a rich man,
    Or if ever I grow to be old,
I will build a house with deep thatch
    To shelter me from the cold,
And there shall the Sussex songs be sung
    And the story of Sussex told.

I will hold my house in the high wood
    Within a walk of the sea,
And the men that were boys when I was a boy
    Shall sit and drink with me.

                           Hilaire Belloc

THE WARDEN OF THE CINQUE PORTS

Written in October, 1852. The Warden was the Duke of Wellington, who died September 13 of the same year.

A mist was driving down the British Channel,
    The day was just begun,
And through the window-panes, on floor and panel.
    Streamed the red autumn sun.

It glanced on flowing flag and rippling pennon,
    And the white sails of ships;
And, from the frowning rampart, the black cannon,
    Hailed it with feverish lips.

Sandwich and Romney, Hastings, Hithe and Dover,
    Were all alert that day,
To see the French war steamers speeding over,
    When the fog cleared away.

Sullen and silent and like couchant lions,
    Their cannon, through the night,
Holding their breath, had watched, in grim defiance
    The sea-coast opposite.

And now they roared at drum-beat through their stations
    On every citadel;
Each answering each, with morning salutations,
    That all was well.

And down the coast, and taking up the burden
    Replied the distant forts,
As if to summon from his sleep the Warden
    And Lord of the Cinque Ports.

Him shall no sunshine from the fields of azure,
  No drum-beat from the wall,
No morning gun from the black fort's embrasure,
  Awaken with its call!

No more, surveying with an eye impartial
  The long line of the coast,
Shall the gaunt figure of the old Field Marshal
  Be seen upon his post!

For in the night, unseen, a single warrior,
  In sombre harness mailed
Dreaded of man, and surnamed the Destroyer,
  The rampart wall had scaled.

He passed into the chamber of the sleeper,
  The dark and silent room;
And as he entered, darker grew and deeper,
  The silence and the gloom.

He did not pause to parley or dissemble
  But smote the Warden hoar
Ah! what a blow, that made all England tremble
  And groan from shore to shore.

Meanwhile, without, the surly cannon waited,
  The sun rose bright o'erhead;
Nothing in Nature's aspect intimated
  That a great man was dead.

Henry Wadsworth Longfellow

AN EVENING IN ENGLAND

From its blue vase the rose of evening drops;
Upon the streams its petals float away.
The hills all blue with distance hide their tops
In the dim silence falling on the grey.
A little wind said "Hush!" and shook a spray
Heavy with May's white crop of opening bloom;
A silent bat went dipping in the gloom.

Night tells her rosary of stars full soon,
They drop from out her dark hand to her knees.
Upon a silhouette of woods, the moon
Leans on one horn as if beseeching ease
From all her changes which have stirred the seas.
Across the ears of Toil, Rest throws her veil.
I and a marsh bird only make a wail.

Francis Ledwidge

NATIONAL AIR

God save our gracious King,
Long live our noble King,
　God save the King!
Send him victorious,
Happy and glorious,
Long to reign over us
　God save the King!

O Lord our God, arise,
Scatter his enemies
　And make them fall!
Confound their politics,
Frustrate their knavish tricks,
On thee our hopes we fix,
　God save the King!

Thy choicest gifts in store,
On him be pleased to pour,
　Long may he reign!
May he defend our laws,
And ever give us cause,
To sing with heart and voice,
　God save the King!

(Words and song attributed to Henry Carey, 1692?)

Ireland

"The Emerald Isle," home of the original Celt, famous for peppery tempers and for political aspirations, for constant fighting and for fiery orators; beloved for beautiful Killarney and for the mountain dew, for the Blarney stone and the happy-go-lucky jaunting car; home of the mystic poet, A. E., and his friend Padraic Colum, of the patriots Robert Emmet and Charles Parnell, and of the good Saint Patrick who was a transplanted Scotchman; on whose stage the Sinn Fein movement has played its stormy drama; the land of fine linen, of thatched cottages, of the shillalah and the festive wake, still dreaming of the "harp that once through Tara's halls"; gay, laughing Ireland, full of poetry and resentment, with a chip on her shoulder and wit on her lips, always ready to fight and then to forgive.

QUEENSTOWN HARBOUR

To Queenstown harbour come great ocean ships
Decked out with flags which the strong sea-wind whips
To prim rigidity, while sea-gulls scream
About the vessel's wake, and puffs of steam
Break from the whistle, as the tender draws away
A throng of passengers: some back to stay
The summer months at home in Kerry, Clare,
Or Cork; others with lordly tourist air
Seek what they've read about—where tourists go:
Killarney; Blarney; Avoca's Vale, Wicklow;
Dublin; Belfast. But they will never see
The vision of great Erin's mystery—
Which even now is hidden in that cloud
Creeping round yonder mountain like a shroud,—
Hear Ireland's wail within the sea-bird's cry.
It is a lovely summer night, and I—
Stand looking from the carriage window; the train
Starts slowly; lights twinkle through the air which rain
Has made the softer, and the hills are changed
To purple, then to black; they seem arranged
By some great child who moulds a map in play.
Darkly the waters glisten; we glide away;
The picture passes and we settle down.
Two hours more,—and then loved Mallow town!

Norreys Jephson O'Conor

THE FAIRY LOUGH

Loughareema! Loughareema
  Lies so high among the heather;
A little lough, a dark lough,
  The wather's black and deep.
Ould herons go a-fishin' there,
  An' sea-gulls all together
Float roun' the one green island
  On the fairy lough asleep.

Loughareema, Loughareema;
  When the sun goes down at seven,
When the hills are dark an' *airy,*
  'Tis a curlew whistles sweet!
Then somethin' rustles all the reeds
  That stand so thick an' even;
A little wave runs up the shore
  An' flees, as if on feet.

Loughareema! Loughareema!
  Stars come out, an' stars are hidin':
The wather whispers on the stones,
  The flitterin' moths are free.
Onc'st before the mornin' light
  The Horsemen will come ridin'
Roun' an' roun' the fairy lough,
  An' no one there to see.

Moira O'Neill

THE WELL OF ALL-HEALING

There's a cure for sorrow in the well at Ballylee
  Where the scarlet cressets hang over the trembling pool:
And joyful winds are blowing from the Land of Youth to
    me,
  And the heart of the earth is full.

Many and many a sunbright maiden saw the enchanted land
  With star faces glimmer up from the druid wave:
Many and many a pain of love was soothed by a faery hand
  Or lost in the love it gave.

When the quiet with a ring of pearl shall wed the earth,
  And the scarlet berries burn dark by the stars in the pool;
Oh, it's lost and deep I'll be amid the Danaan mirth,
  While the heart of the earth is full.

A. E. (George William Russell)

BLARNEY CASTLE

O, did you ne'er hear of "the Blarney"
That's found near the banks of Killarney?
  Believe it from me,
  No girl's heart is free,
Once she hears the sweet sound of the Blarney.

For the Blarney's so great a deceiver,
That a girl thinks you're there, though you leave her;
  And never finds out
  All the tricks you're about
Till she's quite gone herself—with your Blarney.

O say, would you find this same "Blarney"?
There's a castle, not far from Killarney,
  On the top of its wall
  (But take care you don't fall)
There's a stone that contains all this Blarney.

Like a magnet, its influence such is,
That attraction it gives all it touches;
  If you kiss it, they say,
  From that blessed day
You may kiss whom you please with your Blarney.

Samuel Lover

THE BELLS OF SHANDON

Cork, Saint Anne's Church

With deep affection
And recollection
I often think of
  Those Shandon bells,
Whose sounds so wild would,
In the days of childhood,
Fling round my cradle
  Their mystic spells.

On this I ponder
Where'er I wander,
And thus grow fonder,
  Sweet Cork, of thee,—
With thy bells of Shandon,
That sound so grand on
The pleasant waters
  Of the river Lee.

I've heard bells chiming
Full many a clime in,
Toiling sublime in
  Cathedral shrine,
While at a glib rate
Brass tongue would vibrate;
But all their music
  Spoke naught like thine.

For memory, dwelling
On each proud swelling
Of thy belfry, knelling
  Its bold notes free,

Made the bells of Shandon,
Sound far more grand on
The pleasant waters
  Of the river Lee.

I've heard bells tolling
Old Adrian's Mole in
Their thunder rolling
  From the Vatican,—
And cymbals glorious
Swinging uproarious
In the gorgeous turrets
  Of Notre Dame;

But thy sounds were sweeter
Than the dome of Peter
Flings o'er the Tiber,
  Pealing solemnly.
Oh! the bells of Shandon,
Sound far more grand on
The pleasant waters
  Of the river Lee.

There's a bell in Moscow;
While on tower and kiosk O!
In St. Sophia
  The Turkman gets,
And loud in air
Calls men to prayer,
From the tapering summit
  Of tall minarets.

Such empty phantom
I freely grant them;
But there's an anthem
   More dear to me,—
'Tis the bells of Shandon,
That sound so grand on
The pleasant waters
   Of the river Lee.

      Father Prout (*Francis Mahony*)

O'CONNELL BRIDGE

In Dublin town the people see
Gorgeous clouds sail gorgeously,
They are finer, I declare,
Than the clouds of anywhere.

A swirl of blue and red and green,
A stream of blinding gold, a sheen
From silver hill, and pearly ridge
Comes each evening on the bridge.

So when you walk in field look down
Lest you tramp on a daisy's crown,
But in a city look always high
And watch the beautiful clouds go by.

James Stephens

AN OLD WOMAN OF THE ROADS

O, to have a little house!
  To own the hearth and stool and all!
The heaped up sods upon the fire,
  The pile of turf against the wall!

To have a clock with weights and chains
  And pendulum swinging up and down!
A dresser filled with shining delph,
  Speckled and white and blue and brown!

I could be busy all the day
  Clearing and sweeping hearth and floor,
And fixing on their shelf again
  My white and blue and speckled store!

I could be quiet there at night
  Beside the fire and by myself,
Sure of a bed and loth to leave
  The ticking clock and the shining delph!

Och! but I'm weary of mist and dark,
  And roads where there's never a house nor bush,
And tired I am of bog and road,
  And the crying wind and the lonesome hush!

And I am praying to God on high,
  And I am praying Him night and day,
For a little house—a house of my own—
  Out of the wind's and the rain's way!

Padraic Colum

SWEET INNISFALLEN

Sweet Innisfallen, fare thee well,
  May calm and sunshine long be thine!
How fair thou art let others tell,—
  To *feel* how fair shall long be mine.

Sweet Innisfallen, long shall dwell
  In memory's dream that sunny smile,
Which o'er thee on that evening fell,
  When first I saw thy fairy isle.

'Twas light, indeed, too blest for one,
  Who had to turn to paths of care—
Through crowded haunts again to run,
  And leave thee bright and silent there;

No more unto thy shores to come,
  But, on the world's rude ocean tossed,
Dream of thee sometimes, as a home
  Of sunshine he had seen and lost.

Far better in thy weeping hours
  To part from thee, as I do now,
When mist is o'er thy blooming bowers,
  Like sorrow's veil on beauty's brow.

For, though unrivalled still thy grace,
  Thou dost not look, as then, *too* blest,
But thus in shadow seem'st a place
  Where erring man might hope to rest.—

Might hope to rest, and find in thee
　A gloom like Eden's, on the day
He left its shade, when every tree,
　Like thine, hung weeping o'er his way.

Weeping or smiling, lovely isle!
　And all the lovelier for thy tears,
For though but rare thy sunny smile,
　'Tis heaven's own glance when it appears.

Like feeling hearts, whose joys are few,
　But, when indeed they come, divine—
The brightest light the sun e'er threw
　Is lifeless to one gleam of thine!

Thomas Moore

STANZAS FROM "SHAMROCK SONG"

O, the red rose may be fair,
And the lily statelier;
But my shamrock, one in three,
Takes the very heart of me!

Many a lover hath the rose
When June's musk-wind breathes and blows:
And in many a bower is heard
Her sweet praise from bee and bird.

But when summer died last year
Rose and lily died with her;
Shamrock stayeth every day,
Be the winds or gold or grey.

Irish hills, as grey as the dove,
Know the little plant I love;
Warm and fair it mantles them
Stretching down from throat to hem.

And it laughs o'er many a vale,
Sheltered safe from storm and gale;
Sky and sun and stars thereof
Love the gentle plant I love.

Soft it clothes the ruined floor
Of many an abbey, grey and hoar,
And the still home of the dead
With its green is carpeted.

O, the red rose shineth rare,
And the lily saintly fair;
But my shamrock, one in three,
Takes the inmost heart of me!

Katharine Tynan

DUBLIN

Old Dublin City, there is no doubtin'
   Bates every city upon the say.
'Tis there you'd hear O'Connell spoutin'
   And Lady Morgan makin' tay.
For 'tis the capital of the finest nation,
   With charmin' pisintry upon a fruitful sod,
Fightin' like divils for conciliation,
   And hatin' each other for the love of God.

Charles J. Lever

From: "Notes and Queries"

ERIN

When Erin first rose from the dark swelling flood,
God blessed the green island, he saw it was good,
The Emerald of Europe, it sparkled and shone
In the ring of this world, the most precious stone.

William Drennan

From: "Erin"

CUSHLA MA CHREE

Dear Erin, how sweetly thy green bosom rises,
An emerald set in the ring of the sea.
Each blade of thy meadows thy faithful heart prizes,
Thou queen of the west, the world's cushla ma chree.

John Philpot Curran

THE FAIR HILLS OF IRELAND

From the Irish

A plenteous place is Ireland for hospitable cheer,
     Uileacan dubh O!
Where the wholesome fruit is bursting from the yellow bar-
     ley ear;
     Uileacan dubh O!
There is honey in the trees where her misty vales expand,
And her forest paths in summer are by falling waters fann'd
There is dew at high noontide there, and springs i' the yellow
     sand,
  On the fair hills of holy Ireland.

Curl'd he is and ringleted, and plaited to the knee—
     Uileacan dubh O!
Each captain who comes sailing across the Irish Sea;
     Uileacan dubh O!
And I will make my journey, if life and health but stand,
Unto that pleasant country, that fresh and fragrant strand,
And leave your boasted braveries, your wealth and high
     command,
  For the fair hills of holy Ireland.

Large and profitable are the stacks upon the ground,
     Uileacan dubh O!
The butter and the cream do wondrously abound;
     Uileacan dubh O!
The cresses on the water and the sorrels are at hand,
And the cuckoo's calling daily his note of music bland,
And the bold thrush sings so bravely his song i' the forests
     grand,
  On the fair hills of holy Ireland.

Sir Samuel Ferguson

THE LAKE ISLE OF INNISFREE

I will arise and go now, and go to Innisfree,
And a small cabin build there, of clay and wattles made;
Nine bean rows will I have there, a hive for the honey bee,
  And live alone in the bee-loud glade.

And I shall have some peace there, for peace comes drop-
        ping slow,
Dropping from the veils of the morning to where the cricket
        sings;
There midnight's all a glimmer, and noon a purple glow,
        And evening full of the linnet's wings.

I will arise and go now, for always night and day
I hear lake water lapping with low sounds by the shore;
While I stand on the roadway, or on the pavements gray,
  I hear it in the deep heart's core.

William Butler Yeats

CARROWMORE

It's a lonely road through bogland to the lake at Carrow-
    more,
And a sleeper there lies dreaming where the water laps the
    shore;
Though the moth-wings of the twilight in their purples are
    unfurled,
Yet his sleep is filled with music by the masters of the world.

There's a hand is white as silver that is fondling with his
    hair:
There are glimmering feet of sunshine that are dancing by
    him there:
And half-open lips of faery that were dyed a faery red
In their revels where the Hazel Tree its holy clusters shed.

"Come away," the red lips whisper, "all the world is weary
    now;
'Tis the twilight of the ages and it's time to quit the plough.
Oh, the very sunlight's weary ere it lightens up the dew,
And its gold is changed and faded before it falls to you.

"Though your colleen's heart be tender, a tenderer heart
    is near.
What's the starlight in her glances when the stars are
    shining clear?
Who would kiss the fading shadow when the flower face
    glows above?
'Tis the beauty of all Beauty that is calling for your love."

Oh, the great gates of the mountain have opened once again,
And the sound of song and dancing falls upon the ears of
    men,

And the Land of Youth lies gleaming, flushed with rainbow
    light and mirth,
And the old enchantment lingers in the honey-heart of earth.

A. E. (George William Russell)

NATIONAL AIR

Oh! Paddy dear, and did you hear the news that's goin'
    round?
The shamrock is forbid by law to grow on Irish ground,
Saint Patrick's day no more we'll keep, his color can't be
    seen,
For there's a cruel law agin' the wearing of the green!
I met with Napper Tandy and he took me by the hand,
And said he, "How's poor old Ireland and how does she
    stand?"
"She's the most distressful country that ever yet was seen;
They're hanging men and women there for wearing of the
    green."

Then since the color we must wear is England's cruel red,
'Twill serve but to remind us of the blood that has been
    shed;
You may take the shamrock from your hat and cast it on the
    sod
But never fear 'twill take root there though under foot 'tis
    trod.
When laws can stop the blades of grass from growing as
    they grow
And when the leaves in summer time their verdure dare
    not show,
Then I will change the color that I wear in my canteen,
But till that day, please God, I'll stick to wearing of the
    green.

But if at last our color should be torn from Ireland's heart,
Her sons with shame and sorrow from the dear old isle will
      part,
I've heard a whisper of a land that lies beyond the sea
Where rich and poor stand equal in the light of freedom's
      day.
Oh Erin, must we leave you, driven by a tyrant's hand?
Must we ask a mother's blessing from a strange and distant
      land?
Where the cruel cross of England shall never more be seen,
And where, please God, we'll live and die, still wearing of
      the green.

Old Song (about 1798)

Scotland

Land of brose and of Robert Burns, of "Scots wha hae wi' Wallace bled," of Monteith and Montrose, of lovely Mary Stuart and of bonnie Prince Charlie, of those "ladies from Hell" whose kilts and bagpipes made famous the 42d and the Black Watch; home of Harry Lauder and his "roamin' in the gloamin'"; famous for her houghs and lochs, immortalized in song and story; respected for her thrift and for her gifts to the world of statesmen, scholars, millionaires and "meenisters"; land of the straight and narrow path laid down by the stern discipline of John Knox; land of haggis and heather; land of Cosmo Gordon Lang and Ramsay MacDonald, of Geddes and Haig and Barrie and Arthur Balfour; a careful land in settings picturesque.

CHARTLESS

I never saw a moor,
  I never saw the sea;
Yet know I how the heather looks,
  And what a wave must be.

I never spoke with God,
  Nor visited in heaven;
Yet certain am I of the spot
  As if the chart were given.

Emily Dickinson

HEATHER

All my life long I had longed to see heather
  In the land of my kinsmen far over the sea—
Now here is heather like a wide purple ocean
  Rolling its tides toward me,

Dark, dipping waves of it, deeper than amethyst
  When the gold day was begun—
Long, curving swells of it, dusky and lovely,
  Here on the downs in the sun;

Or in a gray mist, sombre and wonderful,
  Like a great twilight outspread
Far over earth that would meet with the heavens
  Purple and wild overhead.

Now I am shaken by great storms of beauty
  Wetting my eyelids with joy of my eyes;
Now is my soul like a wind-stricken sea bird
  Troubling the deep with her cries!

Marguerite Wilkinson

HIGHLAND MARY

Ye banks and braes and streams around
    The castle o' Montgomery,
Green be your woods, and fair your flowers,
    Your waters never drumlie!
There simmer first unfauld her robes,
    And there the langest tarry;
For there I took the last fareweel
    O' my sweet Highland Mary.

How sweetly bloom'd the gay green birk,
    How rich the hawthorn's blossom,
As underneath their fragrant shade
    I clasp'd her to my bosom!
The golden hours on angel wings
    Flew o'er me and my dearie;
For dear to me as light and life
    Was my sweet Highland Mary.

Wi' mony a vow and lock'd embrace
    Our parting was fu' tender;
And pledging aft to meet again,
    We tore oursels asunder;
But, oh! fell Death's untimely frost,
    That nipt my flower sae early!
Now green's the sod, and cauld's the clay,
    That wraps my Highland Mary!

O pale, pale now, those rosy lips,
    I aft hae kiss'd sae fondly!
And closed for aye the sparkling glance
    That dwelt on me sae kindly;

And mouldering now in silent dust
  That heart that lo'ed me dearly;
But still within my bosom's core
  Shall live my Highland Mary.

Robert Burns

EDINBURGH

City of mist and rain and blown gray spaces,
    Dashed with wild wet color and gleam of tears,
Dreaming in Holyrood halls of the passionate faces
    Lifted to one Queen's face that has conquered the years,
Are not the halls of thy memory haunted places?
    Cometh there not as a moon (where the blood-rust sears
Floors a-flutter of old with silks and laces),
    Gliding, a ghostly Queen, through a mist of tears?

Proudly here, with a loftier pinnacled splendor,
    Throned in his northern Athens, what spells remain
Still on the marble lips of the Wizard, and render
    Silent the gazer on glory without a stain!
Here and here, do we whisper, with hearts more tender
    Tusitala wandered through mist and rain;
Rainbow-eyed and frail and gallant and slender,
    Dreaming of pirate-isles in a jewelled main.

Up the Cannongate climbeth, cleft asunder
    Raggedly here, with a glimpse of the distant sea
Flashed through a crumbling alley, a glimpse of wonder,
    Nay, for the City is throned on Eternity!
Hark! from the soaring castle a cannon's thunder
    Closes an hour for the world and an æon for me,
Gazing at last from the martial heights whereunder
    Deathless memories roll to an ageless sea.

Alfred Noyes

EDINBURGH

The Lyric Baedeker

A bonny burgh is Edinbro', the city brave and bright
That spreads in green and gray below the castle on the
       height;
And there on lovely Princes Street the people group in knots
To talk about the latest news of Mary, Queen of Scots.

The castle is a gallant keep and one you're bound to view;
A military pensioner will kindly take you through,
Rehearsing inexhaustibly the plots and counterplots
That made it insalubrious for Mary, Queen of Scots.

You'll see the ancient Canongate; you'll see the house of
       Knox,
With churches here and churches there, all strictly orthodox;
You'll see the works of colorists who lavished paint in pots
On old and recent likenesses of Mary, Queen of Scots.

And when amid the gorse and sheep you've climbed to
       Arthur's Seat
(Where Arthur, says the legend, watched his army in
       retreat),
Your eye shall rest on Holyrood and other noted spots,
Connected with the tragedy of Mary, Queen of Scots.

You'll see the marble statue of the Wizard of the North,
You'll see the cantilever bridge that spans the Firth of
       Forth—
A noble bridge, but when 'twas done the builders cursed
       their lots
Because it wasn't patronized by Mary, Queen of Scots.

[78]

A blessing on the bonny burgh, and all it holds enshrined,
On every house of native rock, on every close and wynd,
And send it good historians to clear whatever blots
May rest upon the memory of Mary, Queen of Scots!

Arthur Guiterman

IN THE HIGHLANDS, IN THE COUNTRY PLACES

In the highlands, in the country places
Where the old plain men have rosy faces,
And the young fair maidens
Quiet eyes;
Where essential silence cheers and blesses,
And forever in the hill-recesses
Her more lovely music broods and dies!
Broods and dies.

O to mount again where erst I haunted;
Where the old red hills are bird-enchanted,
And the low green meadows bright with sward
Bright with sward;
And when even dies the million tinted,
And the night has come, and planets glinted,
Lo! the valley hollow
Lamp-bestarred.

O to dream, O to awake and wander
There, and with delight to take and render,
Through the trance of silence,
Quiet breath;
Lo! for there, among the flowers and grasses,
Only the mightier movement sounds and passes;
Only winds and rivers,
Life and death.

Robert Louis Stevenson

THE LAIRD

Just a wee bit man—five-four in his shoon—
Just a wee bit laird o' a wee bit toon,
Just a great big heart, an' a head that's soon'—
    An' that is the Laird.

Just a wee bit hoose wi' a wee bit ha',
Just a wee bit byre wi' a wee bit sta',
Just a coo, a calf, an' a stirk or twa—
    An' that is the Laird's.

Just a heather hill whaur the sunshine sleeps,
Just a park or twa an' a field o' neeps,
Just as muckle corn as a lassie reaps—
    An' that is the Laird's.

Just a wee bit swine's crue, wi' a grumphy in't,
Just a wee kailyaird, wi' the dung no stint,
Just a patch o' thyme an' o' peppermint—
    An' that is the Laird's.

Just five score o' yowes wi' their lambs run wide,
Just a pair o' horse an' a shalt tae ride,
Just the sweetest wife in the kintra side—
    An' that is the Laird's.

Jeffrey Inglis

LAY OF THE LAST MINSTREL

Canto VI, St. 2

O Caledonia stern and wild
Meet nurse for a poetic child
Land of brown heath and shaggy wood,
Land of the mountain and the flood.

Sir Walter Scott

MELROSE ABBEY

If thou wouldst view fair Melrose aright,
Go visit it by the pale moonlight;
For the gay beams of lightsome day,
Gild, but to flout, the ruins gray.
When the broken arches are black in night,
And each shafted oriel glimmers white;
When the cold light's uncertain shower
Streams on the ruined central tower;
When buttress and buttress, alternately,
Seem framed of ebon and ivory;
When silver edges the imagery,
And the scrolls that teach thee to live and die;
When distant Tweed is heard to rave,
And the owlet to hoot o'er the dead man's grave,
Then go—but go alone the while—
Then view Saint David's ruined pile;
And, home returning, soothly swear,
Was never scene so sad and fair!

Sir Walter Scott

[83]

SCOTLAND

O Scotia, my dear, my native soil
For whom my warmest wish to Heaven is sent
Long may thy hardy sons of rustic toil
Be blest with wealth and peace and sweet content.

Robert Burns

From: "The Cotter's Saturday Night"

THE BANKS O' DOON

Ye flowery banks o' bonie Doon,
  How can ye blume sae fair!
How can ye chant, ye little birds,
  And I sae fu' o' care!

Thou'll break my heart, thou bonie bird,
  That sings upon the bough;
Thou minds me o' the happy days
  When my fause Luve was true.

Thou'll break my heart, thou bonie bird,
  That sings beside thy mate;
For sae I sat, and sae I sang,
  And wistna o' my fate.

Aft hae I roved by bonie Doon,
  To see the woodbine twine;
And ilka bird sang o' its luve,
  And sae did I o' mine.

Wi' lightsome heart I pu'd a rose
  Frae off its thorny tree;
But my fause luver staw my rose,
  And left the thorn wi' me.

Robert Burns

THE TROSACHS

There's not a nook within this solemn Pass
   But were an apt confessional for one
   Taught by his summer spent, his autumn gone,
That Life is but a tale of morning grass
Wither'd at eve. From scenes of art which chase
   That thought away, turn, and with watchful eyes
   Feed it 'mid Nature's old felicities,
Rocks, rivers, and smooth lakes more clear than glass
Untouch'd, unbreathed upon. Thrice happy quest,
   If from a golden perch of aspen spray
   (October's workmanship to rival May)
The pensive warbler of the ruddy breast
   That moral sweeten by a heaven-taught lay,
Lulling the year, with all its cares, to rest!

William Wordsworth

NATIONAL AIR

SCOTLAND

Scots wha hae wi' Wallace bled!
Scots wham Bruce has aften led
Welcome to your gory bed,
  Or to victorie!
Now's the day and now the hour:
See the front of battle lour:
See approach proud Edward's power;
  Chains and slavery!

Wha will be a traitor knave?
Wha can fill a coward's grave?
Wha sae base as be a slave?
  Let him turn and flee!
Wha for Scotland's king and law,
Freedom's sword will strongly draw
Freeman stand, or freeman fa',
  Let him follow me!

By oppression's woes an' pains,
By our sons in servile chains,
We will drain our dearest veins,
  But they shall be free!
Lay the proud usurpers low!
Tyrants fall in ev'ry foe!
Liberty's in every blow!
Let us do or die!

Robert Burns

Wales

Land of Caerleon-on-Usk, of the Eisteddfod with its sweet singers, of careful husbandmen in shadowy vales of the Wye; home of the versatile and volatile Lloyd George; picturesque setting for a people whose sentiments are always independent, but peacefully so.

"OH, LITTLE COUNTRY OF MY HEART"

WALES

Oh, little country of my heart,
  Lying so far beyond the sea,
Far from my land of birth apart,
  And yet so near in thought to me!

Before I saw you with my eyes
  My spirit knew your valleys fair,
Watered by turf-brown streams that rise
  Upon your mountains wild and bare.

Your mountains beautiful and wild
  Where still the fairy people dwell,
While I was but a little child
  In mystic dreams I knew them well.

For of your race a banished part
  Pines like a prisoned bird in me,
Oh, little country of my heart,
  Lying so far beyond the sea!

Mildred Howells

NATIONAL AIR

WALES

Hark, I hear the foe advancing, barbed steeds are proudly
    prancing,
Helmets in the sunbeam glancing, glitter through the trees.
Men of Harlech, lie ye dreaming? See you not their
    falchions gleaming,
While their pennons gaily streaming, flutter to the breeze?
From the rocks rebounding, let the war cry sounding,
Summon all at Cambria's call, the haughty foe surrounding!
Men of Harlech, on to glory; see your banner famed in
    story,
Waves these burning words before ye, "Britain scorns to
    yield"!

Mid the fray see dead and dying, friend and foe together
    lying,
All around the arrows flying, scatter sudden death.
Frightened steeds are wildly neighing, brazen trumpets
    hoarsely braying,
Wounded men for mercy praying, with their parting breath.
See, they're in disorder! comrades, keep close order!
Ever shall they rue the day they ventured o'er the border.
Now the Saxon flies before us, Vict'ry's banner floateth o'er
    us,
Raise the loud exulting chorus, "Britain wins the field!"

                                        Thomas Oliphant

Belgium

A heroic land, made famous by her martyrdom; a land whose dark skies overcloud her cities, but whose courage and industry stand out in bright and blazing colors; within whose borders the traveller finds great mementoes of heroism; a tiny country, of concentrated catastrophes and critical victories.

THE BELFRY OF BRUGES

Carillon

In the ancient town of Bruges,
In the quaint old Flemish city,
As the evening shades descended,
Low and loud and sweetly blended,
Low at times and loud at times,
And changing like a poet's rhymes,
Rang the beautiful wild chimes
From the Belfry in the market
Of the ancient town of Bruges.

Then, with deep sonorous clangor
Calmly answering their sweet anger,
When the wrangling bells had ended,
Slowly struck the clock eleven,
And, from out the silent heaven,
Silence on the town descended.
Silence, silence everywhere,
On the earth and in the air,
Save that footsteps here and there
Of some burgher home returning,
By the street lamps faintly burning,
For a moment woke the echoes
Of the ancient town of Bruges.

But amid my broken slumbers
Still I heard those magic numbers,
As they loud proclaimed the flight
And stolen marches of the night;
Till their chimes in sweet collision
Mingled with each wandering vision,

Mingled with the fortune-telling
Gypsy-bands of dreams and fancies,
Which amid the waste expanses
Of the silent land of trances
Have their solitary dwelling;
All else seemed asleep in Bruges,
In the quaint old Flemish city.

And I thought how like these chimes
Are the poet's airy rhymes,
All his rhymes and roundelays,
His conceits, and songs, and ditties,
From the belfry of his brain,
Scattered downward, though in vain,
On the roofs and stones of cities!
For by night the drowsy ear
Under its curtains cannot hear,
And by day men go their ways,
Hearing the music as they pass,
But deeming it no more, alas!
Than the hollow sound of brass.

Yet perchance a sleepless wight,
Lodging at some humble inn
In the narrow lanes of life,
When the dusk and hush of night
Shut out the incessant din
Of daylight and its toil and strife,
May listen with a calm delight
To the poet's melodies,
Till he hears, or dreams he hears,
Intermingled with the song,
Thoughts that he has cherished long;

Hears amid the chime and singing
The bells of his own village ringing,
And wakes, and finds his slumberous eyes
Wet with most delicious tears.

Thus dreamed I, as by night I lay
In Bruges, at the Fleur-de-Blé,
Listening with a wild delight
To the chimes that, through the night,
Rang their changes from the Belfry
Of that quaint old Flemish city.

Henry Wadsworth Longfellow

THE BELFRY OF BRUGES

In the market-place of Bruges stands the belfry old and
     brown;
Thrice consumed and thrice rebuilded, still it watches o'er
     the town.

As the summer morn was breaking, on that lofty tower I
     stood,
And the world threw off its darkness, like the weeds of
     widowhood.

Thick with towns and hamlets studded, and with streams
     and vapors gray,
Like a shield embossed with silver, round and vast the
     landscape lay.

At my feet the city slumbered. From its chimneys, here and
     there,
Wreaths of snow-white smoke, ascending, vanished, ghost-
     like, into air.

Not a sound rose from the city at that early morning hour,
But I heard a heart of iron beating in the ancient tower.

From their nests beneath the rafters sang the swallows wild
     and high
And the world, beneath me sleeping, seemed more distant
     than the sky.

Then most musical and solemn, bringing back the olden
     times,
With their strange, unearthly changes, rang the melancholy
     chimes.

Like the psalms from some old cloister, when the nuns sing
    in the choir;
And the great bell tolled among them, like the chanting of
    a friar.

Visions of the days departed, shadowy phantoms filled my
    brain;
They who live in history only seemed to walk the earth
    again;

All the Foresters of Flanders,—mighty Baldwin Bras de
    Fer,
Lyderick du Bucq and Cressy, Philip, Guy de Dampierre.

I beheld the pageants splendid that adorned those days of
    old;
Stately dames, like queens attended, knights who bore the
    Fleece of Gold;

Lombard and Venetian merchants with deep-laden argosies;
Ministers from twenty nations; more than royal pomp and
    ease.

I beheld proud Maximilian, kneeling humbly on the ground;
I beheld the gentle Mary, hunting with her hawk and
    hound;

And her lighted bridal-chamber, where a duke slept with
    the queen,
And the armèd guard around them, and the sword
    unsheathed between.

I beheld the Flemish weavers, with Namur and Juliers bold,
Marching homeward from the bloody battle of the Spurs
    of Gold;

Saw the fight at Minnewater, saw the White Hoods moving
    west,
Saw great Artevelde victorious scale the Golden Dragon's
    nest.

And again the whiskered Spaniard all the land with terror
    smote;
And again the wild alarum sounded from the tocsin's throat;

Till the bell of Ghent responded o'er lagoon and dike of
    sand,
"I am Roland! I am Roland! there is victory in the land!"

Then the sound of drums aroused me. The awakened city's
    roar
Chased the phantoms I had summoned back into their graves
    once more.

Hours had passed away like minutes; and, before I was
    aware,
Lo! the shadow of the belfry crossed the sun-illumined
    square.

Henry Wadsworth Longfellow

NATIONAL AIR

BELGIUM

Who'd have believed such self-willed daring, that his base
     end he might attain,
Avid for blood, a prince unsparing, bullets on us should
     rain?
Let it end! Belgians, be free men! From Nassau brook no
     more indignity
Since Grape has torn down the Orange flying, upon the
     tree of Liberty!
Upon the tree of Liberty, upon the tree of Liberty!

In gen'rous wrath all too forbearant, Belgium strove for a
     righteous cause.
She from her king, as from a parent, only asked juster laws,
But 'twas he who with furious folly, with guns his son
     loosed on us ruthlessly
With Belgian blood stained the flag of Orange, upon the
     tree of Liberty,
Upon the tree of Liberty, upon the tree of Liberty!

Brabanters proud with hearts courageous, who in battle are
     e'er so brave!
You from Batavia's yoke outrageous, ball and powder shall
     save!
At the feet of the Archangel, o'er Brussels then shall your
     flag float free,
And proudly flourish without the Orange, upon the tree of
     Liberty,
Upon the tree of Liberty, upon the tree of Liberty!

                         François van Campenhout

Holland

A small land, personifying patience, fighting a mighty enemy, the sea, and ever watchful of its encroachments; a land of power and wealth, none the less; home of the Pilgrim Fathers, of toleration and freedom; a land of canals and spotless cleanliness; a blooming garden of flowers and fruit and vegetables, which every morning feeds the English nation; a land where quaint cities border the canals, and wooden shoes clatter along the streets; famous for its great artists, Rembrandt, Israels, Ruisdael and Frans Hals; noted for mountains of Edam cheese and armies of sturdy babies; the land of refuge for all the persecuted of the world despite its fight with dykes and drains against the sea; a land where restless windmills guard a peaceful people, earning their wealth by patient effort.

THE HEAVENLY HILLS OF HOLLAND

The heavenly hills of Holland,—
  How wondrously they rise
Above the smooth green pastures
  Into the azure skies!
With blue and purple hollows,
  With peaks of dazzling snow,
Along the far horizon
  The clouds are marching slow.

No mortal foot has trodden
  The summits of that range,
Nor walked those mystic valleys
  Whose colors ever change;
Yet we possess their beauty,
  And visit them in dreams,
While the ruddy gold of sunset
  From cliff and canyon gleams.

In days of cloudless weather
  They melt into the light;
When fog and mist surround us
  They're hidden from our sight;
But when returns a season
  Clear shining after rain,
While the northwest wind is blowing,
  We see the hills again.

The old Dutch painters loved them,
  Their pictures show them clear,—
Old Hobbema and Ruysdael,
  Van Goyen and Vermeer.

Above the level landscape,
    Rich polders, long-armed mills,
Canals and ancient cities,—
    Float Holland's heavenly hills.

Henry van Dyke

GOING TOO FAR

A woman who lived in Holland, of old,
Polished her brass till it shone like gold.
She washed her pig after all his meals
In spite of his energetic squeals.
She scrubbed her doorstep into the ground,
And the children's faces, pink and round,
She washed so hard that in several cases
She polished their features off their faces—
Which gave them an odd appearance, though
She thought they were really neater so!
Then her passion for cleaning quickly grew,
And she scrubbed and polished the village through,
Until, to the rage of all the people,
She cleaned the weather-vane off the steeple.
As she looked at the sky one summer's night
She thought that the stars shone out less bright;
And she said with a sigh, "If I were there,
I'd rub them up till the world should stare."
That night a storm began to brew,
And a wind from the ocean blew and blew
Till, when she came to her door next day
It whisked her up, and blew her away—
Up and up in the air so high
That she vanished, at last, in the stormy sky.
Since then it's said that each twinkling star
And the big white moon, shine brighter far.
But the neighbors shake their heads in fear
She may rub so hard they will disappear!

Mildred Howells

NIGHTFALL IN DORDRECHT

The mill goes toiling slowly around
   With steady and solemn creak
And my little one hears in the kindly sound
   The voice of the old mill speak.
While round and round those big white wings
   Grimly and ghostlike creep,
My little one hears that the old mill sings,
   "Sleep, little tulip, sleep!"

The sails are reefed and the nets are drawn,
   And, over his pot of beer,
The fisher, against the morrow's dawn
   Lustily maketh cheer.
He mocks at the winds that caper along
   From the far-off clamorous deep—
But we—we love their lullaby song
   Of "Sleep, little tulip, sleep!"

Old dog Fritz in slumber sound
   Groans of the stony mart:
To-morrow how proudly he'll trot you round,
   Hitched to our new milk cart.
And you shall help me blanket the kine
   And fold the gentle sheep,
And set the herring a-soak in brine—
   But now, little tulip, sleep!

A Dream-one comes to button the eyes
   That wearily droop and blink,
While the old mill buffets the frowning skies
   And scolds at the stars that wink;

Over your face the misty wings
　　Of that beautiful Dream-one sweep,
And rocking your cradle, she softly sings,
　　"Sleep, little tulip, sleep!"

Eugene Field

NATIONAL AIR

Let all with Dutch blood in their veins, whose love of home
is strong,
Now help to raise th' inspiring strains and praise our Prince
in song.
With noble thought lift up one voice, united heart and
hand,
God bids our hearts in song rejoice, for Prince and Father-
land,
For Prince and Fatherland.

We're brothers true, unto a man, we sing the old song
yet,
Away with him who ever can, his Prince or land for-
get;
A human heart glowed in him ne'er, we turn him from
our hand
Who hears unmoved the song and prayer, for Prince and
Fatherland,
For Prince and Fatherland.

Preserve, oh God the hallowed ground, our patriot fathers
gave,
The land where we a cradle found, wherein we'll find a
grave.
We call to thee, oh Lord on high, when near death's door
we stand;
We seek thy blessing, hear our cry, oh Prince and Father-
land,
Oh Prince and Fatherland.

Loud rings through our rejoicings here, our prayer, oh
   Lord, to thee.
Preserve our Prince, his home so dear, to Holland, great
   and free!
From youth through life be this our song, till near to death
   we stand,
Oh God, preserve our sovereign long, our Prince and
   Fatherland,
   Our Prince and Fatherland.

Smits

France

Mecca of the artistic and the fashionable world; famous for its intellectual vigor, for the Louvre, for Notre Dame, for the Sorbonne, for its opalescent atmosphere, for its pot-au-feu; noted for its men of letters, Voltaire, Dumas, Rousseau, Balzac, Racine, Corneille, Molière, Victor Hugo, Anatole France, and for the mad poet, Villon; for its Gothic cathedrals, its beautiful cities, its thrifty peasants, its gay shops; for the splendor of the reign of the Grand Monarque, and the horror of the reign of terror; for Richelieu and for Emperor Napoleon; a land of which it is said that every man has two countries, France and his own; a land whose capital is Paris, and whose name has echoed in glory round the world

EVENING ON CALAIS BEACH

It is a beauteous evening, calm and free,
  The holy time is quiet as a Nun
  Breathless with adoration; the broad sun
Is sinking down in its tranquillity;
The gentleness of heaven broods o'er the sea;
  Listen! the mighty Being is awake,
  And doth with his eternal motion make
A sound like thunder—everlastingly.
Dear Child! dear Girl! that walkest with me here,
  If thou appear untouch'd by solemn thought,
  Thy nature is not therefore less divine:
Thou liest in Abraham's bosom all the year;
  And worshipp'st at the Temple's inner shrine,
  God being with thee when we know it not.

William Wordsworth

PARIS

First, London, for its myriads; for its height,
Manhattan heaped in towering stalagmite;
But Paris for the smoothness of the paths
That lead the heart unto the heart's delight. . . .

Fair loiterer on the threshold of those days
When there's no lovelier prize the world displays
Than, having beauty and your twenty years,
You have the means to conquer and the ways,

And coming where the crossroads separate
And down each vista glories and wonders wait,
Crowning each path with pinnacles so fair
You know not which to choose, and hesitate—

Oh, go to Paris. . . . In the midday gloom
Of some old quarter take a little room
That looks off over Paris and its towers
From Saint Gervais round to the Emperor's Tomb,—

So high that you can hear a mating dove
Croon down the chimney from the roof above,
See Notre Dame and know how sweet it is
To wake between Our Lady and our love.

And have a little balcony to bring
Fair plants to fill with verdure and blossoming,
That sparrows seek, to feed from pretty hands,
And swallows circle over in the Spring.

There of an evening you shall sit at ease
In the sweet month of flowering chestnut-trees,

There with your little darling in your arms,
Your pretty dark-eyed Manon or Louise.

And looking out over the domes and towers
That chime the fleeting quarters and the hours,
While the bright clouds banked eastward back of them
Blush in the sunset, pink as hawthorn flowers,

You cannot fail to think, as I have done,
Some of life's ends attained, so you be one
Who measures life's attainment by the hours
That Joy has rescued from oblivion.

Alan Seeger

PLACE DE LA BASTILLE, PARIS

How dear the sky has been above this place!
Small treasures of this sky that we see here
Seen weak through prison-bars from year to year;
Eyed with a painful prayer upon God's grace
To save, and tears that stayed not long upon the face
Lifted at sunset. Yea, how passing dear,
Those nights when through the bars a wind left clear
The heaven, and moonlight soothed the limpid space!

So was it, till one night the secret kept
Safe in low vault and stealthy corridor
Was blown abroad on gospel-tongues of flame.
O ways of God, mysterious evermore!
How many on this spot have cursed and wept
That all might stand here now and own thy name.

D. G. Rossetti

A TOUR THROUGH FRANCE

Stanza 12

When you've walked up the Rue de la Paix at Paris,
Been to the Louvre and the Tuileries
And to Versailles, although to go so far is
A thing not quite consistent with your ease,
And—but the mass of objects quite a bar is
To my describing what the traveller sees.
You who have ever been to Paris know,
And you who have not been to Paris—go.

John Ruskin

THE VENUS OF MILO

What art thou? Woman? Goddess? Aphrodite?
Yet never such as thou from the cold foam
Of ocean, nor from cloudy heaven might come,
Who wast begotten on her bridal night
In passionate Earth's womb by Man's delight,
When Man was young. I cannot trace in thee
Time's handiwork. Say, rather, where is he
For whom thy face was red which is so white?
Thou standest ravished, broken, and thy face
Is writ with ancient passions. Thou art dumb
To my new love. Yet whatso'er of good,
Of crime, of pride, of passion, or of grace
In woman is, thou, woman, hast in sum.
Earth's archetypal Eve. All Womanhood.

Wilfrid Scawen Blunt

THE WINGED VICTORY

Thou dear and most high Victory,
Whose home is the unvanquished sea,
Whose fluttering wind-blown garments keep
The very freshness, fold and sweep
They wore upon the galley's prow,
By what unwonted favor now
Hast thou alighted in this place,
Thou Victory of Samothrace?

O thou to whom in countless lands
With eager hearts and striving hands
Strong men in their last need have prayed
Greatly desiring, undismayed,
And thou hast been across the fight
Their consolation and their might,
Withhold not now one dearer grace,
Thou Victory of Samothrace!

Behold, we too must cry to thee,
Who wage our strife with Destiny,
And give for beauty and for truth
Our love, our valor and our youth.
Are there no honors for these things
To match the pageantries of kings?
Are we more laggard in the race
Than those who fell at Samothrace?

Not only for the bow and sword
O Victory, be thy reward!
The hands that work with paint and clay
In Beauty's service, shall not they

Also with mighty faith prevail?
Let hope not die, nor courage fail
But joy come with thee pace for pace
As once long since in Samothrace.

Grant us the skill to shape the form
And spread the color living-warm
(As they who wrought aforetime did)
Where love and wisdom shall lie hid,
In fair impassioned types, to sway
The cohorts of the world to-day,
In Truth's eternal cause, and trace
Thy glory down from Samothrace.

With all the ease and splendid poise
Of one who triumphs without noise,
Wilt thou not teach us to attain
Thy sense of power without strain,
That we a little may possess
Our souls with thy sure loveliness,—
That calm the years cannot deface,
Thou Victory of Samothrace?

Then in the ancient, ceaseless war
With infamy, go thou before!
Amid the shoutings and the drums
Let it be learned that Beauty comes,
Man's matchless Paladin to be,
Whose rule shall make his spirit free
As thine from all things mean or base,
Thou Victory of Samothrace!

Bliss Carman

ON THE TOILET TABLE OF QUEEN
MARIE-ANTOINETTE

This was her table, these her trim outspread
Brushes and trays and porcelain cups for red;
Here sat she, while her women tired and curled
The most unhappy head in all the world.

J. B. B. Nichols

THE BOOK-STALLS ON THE SEINE

When you're in Paris next, just after rain—
Whene'er the sun comes out (Give God the praise!)—
Go down and watch their varied owners raise
The covers of the book-stalls on the Seine.

Then watch some stooping scholar, who would fain,
Among worn texts of Greek and Latin plays,
Discover what he's longed for all his days, —
A book so rare he doubts if one remain.

He's scanned two hundred titles line by line,
And failed again. But look! His eyes shine bright:
He's found it! Published by . . . yes, all is right:
The date is fifteen hundred thirty-nine.

And thus you know that Paris is the home
Of Abelard and Bernard—and not Rome.

Charles Lewis Slattery

IN THE GALLERIES OF THE LOUVRE

Among the pictures in these palace halls
One scene which holds me fast with charmed grace
Is of a poor Dutch room, with chimney-place.
There by a window, through which twilight falls

Sits blessed Mary, whom her child enthralls
With His sweet smile and with His fond embrace:
The glowing hearth lights up her joyous face;
From heaven calm sleep, with crooning song she calls.

Is this Dutch scene the home of Christ the King—
The infant of far-distant Palestine?
Yea, Holy Child, for all the earth is Thine,
Round every mother's neck Thy fingers cling;

And what Thy loving mother sang to Thee
Is sung by mothers through eternity.

Charles Lewis Slattery

NOTRE DAME

Often at evening, when the summer sun,
Floats like a gold balloon above the roofs,
I climb this silent tower of Notre Dame—
My sole companion Hugo's deathless book—
For here all limits vanish, here my soul
Breathes and expands, and knows a wider life.
Here in the lustrous, shimmering sunset hour
Painter and poet both might find new words,
New colours, seeing opened in the sky
The jewel-casket of Ithuriel—
Sapphires, cornelians, opals! Pictures here
Are seen, so gorgeous and so rich in hue
That Titian's and Rubens' colouring
Grows pale in memory; and here are built
Misty cathedrals, wonderfully arched,
Mountains of smoke, fantastic colonnades—
All doubled in the mirror of the Seine. . . .
Now comes a breeze which moulds the tattered clouds
Into a thousand new and changing forms,
Mysterious and vague; the passing day,
As if for his good-night, reclothes the church
In vesture of a richer, purer tint.
Her tall twin-towers—those canticles in stone—
Drawn with great strokes upon the fiery sky,
Seem like two mighty arms upraised in pray'r
To God by Paris ere she sinks to sleep.

But ah! when in the darkness you have climbed
The slender spiral staircase, when at last
You see again the blue sky overhead,
The void above you, the abyss below,

Then are you seized by dizziness and fear
Sublime, to feel yourself so close to God.
Even as a branch beneath a perching bird,
The tower shrinks 'neath the pressure of your feet,
Trembles and thrills; th' intoxicated sky
Waltzes and reels around you; the abyss
Opens its jaws: the imp of dizziness,
Flapping you with his wings, leaps mockingly,
And all the parapets shudder and shake.
Weathercocks, spires, and pointed roofs move past
Your dazzled eyes, outlined in silhouette
Against the whirling sky, and in the gulf
Where the apocalyptic raven wheels,
Far down, lies Paris, howling—yet unheard!
O, how the heart beats now! To dominate
With feeble human eye from this great height
A city so immense! With one swift glance
To embrace this mighty whole, standing so near
To Heaven, and beholding, even as
A soaring mountain-eagle, far, far down
In the depth of the crater's heart, the writhing smoke,
The boiling lava! . . .

And yet, O Notre Dame, though Paris robed
In flame-like vesture is so beautiful,
Her beauty vanishes if one should leave
Thy towers and reach the level earth again.
All fades and changes then; nought grand is left
Save only thee. . . . For O, within thy walls
The Lord God makes His Dwelling! Through thy dark
And shadowy places Heaven's angels move,
And light thee with reflections from their wings.
O, world of poetry in this world of prose!

At sight of thee a knocking at the heart
Is felt, a perfect faith makes pure the soul.
When evening damascenes thee with her gold,
And in the dingy square thou, gleaming, stand'st
Like a huge monstrance on a purple dais,
I can believe that by a miracle
Between thy towers the Lord might show Himself. . . .
How small our bourgeois monuments appear
Beside thy Gallic majesty! No dome,
No spire, however proud, can vie with thee—
Thou seem'st indeed to strike against the sky!
Who could prefer, e'en in pedantic taste,
These poor bare Grecian styles, these Panthéons,
These antique fripperies, perishing with cold,
And scarcely knowing how to stand upright,
To the demure, straight folds of thy chaste robe? . . .

Théophile Gautier

(Translated by Eva M. Martin)

WHEN I SET OUT FOR LYONNESSE

When I set out for Lyonnesse,
  A hundred miles away,
  The rime was on the spray,
And starlight lit my lonesomeness
When I set out for Lyonnesse
  A hundred miles away.

What would bechance at Lyonnesse
  While I should sojourn there
  No prophet durst declare,
Nor did the wisest wizard guess
What would bechance at Lyonnesse
  While I should sojourn there.

When I came back from Lyonnesse
  With magic in my eyes,
  All marked with mute surmise
My radiance rare and fathomless,
When I came back from Lyonnesse
  With magic in my eyes!

Thomas Hardy

THE RHONE

Thou Royal River, born of sun and shower
In chambers purple with the Alpine glow,
Wrapped in the spotless ermine of the snow
And rocked by tempests.

Henry Wadsworth Longfellow

From: "The River Rhone"

THE WINES OF FRANCE

The wines of France! The wines of France!
That vivid Villon sipped and sung,
That gave the lure to lady's glance
And loosened royal lover's tongue,
Eternal summer warms them yet!
Alas, for us their sun is set.

The Burgundy and Bordeaux wine
That made Molière and Voltaire gay,
Across our seagirt Volstead line
"They shall not pass," stern Solons say.
What wonder Pegasus is sick?
The winged horse has lost his kick!

The wines of France! The wines of France!
The wines of Marne, Moselle and Seine,
The sacred catacombs of Reims,
The storied hillsides of Champagne,
Lafite, Cote d'Or, Chateau Yquem,
Torment me not with talk of them!

Fill high the bowl with coffee weak
We must not think of themes like these
'Twas wine gave Cyrano his beak . . .
Boy, bring me an egg chocolate, please!
Wine gave Rabelais his ruffian wit.
Boy, bring me a banana split!

Keith Preston

THE NAME OF FRANCE

Give us a name to fill the mind
With the shining thoughts that lead mankind,
The glory of learning, the joy of art,—
A name that tells of a splendid part
In the long, long toil and the strenuous fight
Of the human race to win its way
From the feudal darkness into the day
Of Freedom, Brotherhood, Equal Right,—
A name like a star, a name of light.
  I give you *France!*

Give us a name to stir the blood
With a warmer glow and a swifter flood,—
A name like the sound of a trumpet, clear,
And silver-sweet, and iron-strong,
That calls three million men to their feet,
Ready to march, and steady to meet
The foes who threaten that name with wrong,—
A name that rings like a battle-song.
  I give you *France!*

Give us a name to move the heart
With the strength that noble griefs impart,
A name that speaks of the blood outpoured
To save mankind from the sway of the sword,—
A name that calls on the world to share
In the burden of sacrificial strife
Where the cause at stake is the world's free life
And the rule of the people everywhere,—
A name like a vow, a name like a prayer.
  I give you *France!*

Henry van Dyke

AIX-LA-CHAPELLE

The Tomb of Charlemagne

I stood in that cathedral old, the work of kingly power,
That from the clustered roofs of Aix lifts up its mouldering
    tower.
And, like a legend strange and rude, speaks of an earlier
    day,—
Of saint and knight, the tourney's pomp, and the Minne-
    singer's lay!

Above me rose the pillared dome, with many a statue grim,
And through the chancel-oriel came a splendor soft and dim,
Till dusky shrine and painting old glowed in the lustre wan:
Below me was a marble slab,—the tomb of Charlemagne.

A burst of organ-music rang so grandly, sadly slow,
It seemed a requiem thundered o'er the dead who slept
    below;
And with the sound came thronging round the stern men
    of that time,
When best was he who bravest fought, and cowardice was
    crime.

I thought upon the day when he, whose dust I stood upon,
Ruled with a monarch's boundless right the kingdoms he had
    won,—
When rose the broad Alps in his realm, and roared the
    Baltic's wave;
And now—the lowest serf might stand, unheeded, on his
    grave.

And ruthless hands despoiled his dust, attired in regal pride,
The crown upon his crumpled brows, and Joyeuse by his
    side,—
Whose rusted blade, at Ronceval, flamed in the hero's hand
In answer to the silver horn of the Paladin, Roland.

I stood on that neglected stone, thrilled with the glorious
    sound,
While bowed at many a holier shrine the worshippers
    around,—
And through the cloud of incense-smoke burned many a
    taper dim,
And priestly stoles went sweeping by,—I could but think of
    him!

I saw the boy with yellow locks, crowned at St. Deny's
    shrine;
The emperor in his purple cloak, the lord of all the Rhine;
The conquerer of a thousand foes, in battle stern and hard;
The widowed mourner at thy tomb, O fairest Hildegarde!

Long pealed the music of the choir through chancel-arch
    and nave,
As, lost in those old memories, I stood upon his grave;
And when the morning anthem ceased, and solemn mass
    began,
I left that minster gray and old,—the tomb of Charlemagne!

Bayard Taylor

SAINT OF FRANCE

Wide, restless grey like two bewildered birds
Her eyes were troubled with some nameless quest.
She had heard voices and she could not rest;
She had heard voices crying without words.
And she rose up, and left her father's herds,
And took the path to the hill's blazing crest
And stood, a crimson cross against the west
An instant, and her eyes were homing birds.

She had found peace, and when she came to die
She heard the voices calling her again. . . .
The crackling faggots smouldered on the sky,
And she had made a miracle of pain.
But people who had come to see her die
Remembered only fire and the sky.

Joseph Auslander

IN OLD ROUEN

In old Rouen, where past and present meet,
A mighty duke once reigned—a girl was burned;
And still their shades in boulevard and street
Or some dim crypt or tower may be discerned.

And one has outlines very blurred and faint,
And one has gathered glory from the years;—
Ah, it is not the Conqueror, but the Saint,
Who holds a world's remembrance—through its tears.

Antoinette Decoursey Patterson

THE BALLAD OF BOUILLABAISSE

A street there is in Paris famous,
    For which no rhyme our language yields,
Rue Neuve des Petits Champs its name is—
    The New Street of the Little Fields;
And here's an inn, not rich and splendid,
    But still in comfortable case—
The which in youth I oft attended,
    To eat a bowl of Bouillabaisse.

This Bouillabaisse a noble dish is,
    A sort of soup, or broth, or brew,
Or hotchpotch of all sorts of fishes,
    That Greenwich never could outdo;
Green herbs, red peppers, mussels, saffron,
    Soles, onions, garlic, roach, and dace:
All these you eat at Terré's tavern,
    In that one dish of Bouillabaisse.

Indeed, a rich and savoury stew 'tis:
    And true philosophers, methinks,
Who love all sorts of natural beauties,
    Should love good victuals and good drinks.
And Cordelier or Benedictine
    Might gladly, sure, his lot embrace,
Nor find a fast-day too afflicting,
    Which served him up a Bouillabaisse.

I wonder if the house still there is?
    Yes, here the lamp is, as before;
The smiling, red-cheeked écaillère is
    Still opening oysters at the door.

Is Terré still alive and able?
    I recollect his droll grimace;
He'd come and smile before your table
    And hoped you liked your Bouillabaisse.

We enter; nothing's changed or older.
"How's Monsieur Terré, waiter, pray?"
The waiter stares and shrugs his shoulder:
    "Monsieur is dead this many a day."
"It is the lot of saint and sinner.
    So honest Terré's run his race!"
"What will Monsieur require for dinner!"
    "Say, do you still cook Bouillabaisse?"

"O, oui, Monsieur," 's the waiter's answer;
    "Quel vin Monsieur désire-t-il?"
"Tell me a good one." "That I can, sir;
    The Chambertin with yellow seal."
"So Terré's gone," I say, and sink in
    My old accustomed corner-place;
"He's done with feasting and with drinking,
    With Burgundy and Bouillabaisse."

My old accustomed corner here is,
    The table still is in the nook;
Ah! vanished many a busy year is,
    This well-known chair since last I took.
When first I saw ye, *Cari luoghi,*
    I'd scarce a beard upon my face,
And now a grizzled, grim old fogy,
    I sit and wait for Bouillabaisse.

Where are you, old companions trusty
    Of early days here met to dine?

[138]

Come, waiter! quick, a flagon crusty,—
  I'll pledge them in the good old wine.
The kind old voices and old faces
  My memory can quick retrace;
Around the board they take their places,
  And share the wine and Bouillabaisse.

There's Jack has made a wondrous marriage;
  There's laughing Tom is laughing yet;
There's brave Augustus drives his carriage;
  There's poor old Fred in the Gazette;
On James's head the grass is growing:
  Good Lord! the world has wagged apace
Since here we set the claret flowing,
  And drank, and ate the Bouillabaisse.

Ah me! how quick the days are flitting!
  I mind me of a time that's gone,
When here I'd sit, as now I'm sitting,
  In this same place—but not alone.
A fair young form was nestled near me,
  A dear, dear face looked fondly up,
And sweetly spoke and smiled to cheer me—
  There's no one now to share my cup.

I drink it as the Fates ordain it.
  Come, fill it, and have done with rhymes;
Fill up the lonely glass, and drain it
  In memory of the dear old times.
Welcome the wine, whate'er the seal is;
  And sit you down and say your grace
With thankful heart, whate'er the meal is,—
  Here comes the smoking Bouillabaisse!

William Makepeace Thackeray

[139]

AN OLD CASTLE

The gray arch crumbles
And totters and tumbles;
The bat has built in the banquet hall;
In the donjon-keep
Sly mosses creep;
The ivy has scaled the southern wall.
No man-at-arms
Sounds quick alarms
A-top of the cracked martello tower;
The drawbridge-chain
Is broken in twain—
The bridge will neither rise nor lower.
Not any manner
Of broidered banner
Flaunts at a blazoned herald's call.
Lilies float
In the stagnant moat;
And fair they are, and tall.

Here, in the old
Forgotten springs,
Was wassail held by queens and kings;
Here at the board
Sat clown and lord,
Maiden fair and lover bold,
Baron fat and minstrel lean,
The prince with his stars,
The knight with his scars,
The priest in his gabardine.

Where is she,
Of the fleur-de-lys,
And that true knight who wore her gages?
Where are the glances
That bred wild fancies
In curly heads of my lady's pages?
Where are those
Who, in steel or hose,
Held revel here, and made them gay?
Where is the laughter
That shook the rafter—
Where is the rafter, by the way?
Gone is the roof
And perched aloof
Is an owl, like a friar of Orders Grey.
(Perhaps 'tis the priest,
Come back to feast—
He hath ever a tooth for capon, he!
But the capon's cold
And the steward's old
And the butler's lost the larder-key!)
The doughty lords
Sleep the sleep of swords;
Dead are the dames and damozels;
The King in his crown
Hath laid him down
And the jester with his bells.

All is dead here,
Poppies are red here,
Vines in my lady's chamber grow—
If 'twas her chamber

Where they clamber
Up from the poisonous weeds below.
All is dead here,
Joy is fled here,
Let us hence. 'Tis the end of all—
The gray arch crumbles
And totters and tumbles,
And Silence sits in the banquet hall.

Thomas Bailey Aldrich

CARCASSONNE

How old I am! I'm eighty years!
I've worked both hard and long,
Yet patient all my life has been,
One dearest sight I have not seen,—
It almost seems a wrong;
A dream I had when life was new,
Alas! our dreams! they come not true;
I thought to see fair Carcassonne,—
That lovely city—Carcassonne!

One sees it dimly from the height
Beyond the mountains blue
Fain would I walk five weary leagues,—
I do not mind the road's fatigues,—
Through morn and evening's dew.
But bitter frosts would fall at night
And on the grapes—that yellow blight.
I could not go to Carcassonne,
I never went to Carcassonne.

They say it is as gay all times
As holidays at home!
The gentles ride in gay attire
And in the sun each gilded spire
Shoots up like those at Rome!
The Bishop the procession leads,
The generals curb their prancing steeds,
Alas! I know not Carcassonne,—
Alas! I know not Carcassonne.

Our Vicar's right! he preaches loud,
And bids us to beware;
He says, 'O guard the weakest part,
And most the traitor in the heart
Against Ambition's snare!'
Perhaps in autumn I can find
Two sunny days with gentle wind.
I then could go to Carcassonne,
I still could go to Carcassonne!

My God and Father! pardon me
If this my wish offends!
One sees some hope, more high than he,
In age as in his infancy,
To which his heart ascends.
My wife, my son, have seen Narbonne,
My grandson went to Perpignan;
But I have not seen Carcassonne,—
But I have not seen Carcassonne!

Thus sighed a peasant bent with age
Half dreaming in his chair;
I said, "My friend, come go with me
To-morrow; then thine eyes shall see
Those streets that seem so fair."
That night there came for passing soul
The church-bell's low and solemn toll.
He never saw gay Carcassonne.
Who has not known a Carcassonne?

Gustave Nadaud

AT CARCASSONNE

The years are but a passing sigh,
A garment fretted by a moth,
Yet woven here in tapestry
Are Roman, Saracen, and Goth,
And English knight and Spanish don
At Carcassonne—At Carcassonne.

Along its haunted battlements,
Go belted lords, and ladies fair,
Moving with ghostly elegance
To take the evening air;
For magic comes at setting sun
In Carcassonne—In Carcassonne.

An elfin trumpet sounds a note,
The silence jangles with alarms,
The drawbridge lifts above the moat,
The streets are full of men-at-arms
And Raymond flaunts his gonfalon,
At Carcassonne—At Carcassonne.

Some love the loneliness of down,
And some, a villa by the sea,
And some, the noise of London town,
And some, the nights of gay Paree,
But I have set my heart upon
Old Carcassonne—Old Carcassonne.

George Craig Stewart

NATIONAL AIR

The Marseillaise

Ye sons of freedom, wake to glory!
    Hark! hark! what myriads bid you rise!
Your children, wives, and grandsires hoary,
    Behold their tears and hear their cries!
Shall hateful tyrants, mischief breeding,
    With hireling hosts, a ruffian band,
    Affright and desolate the land,
While peace and liberty lie bleeding?
    To arm! to arms, ye brave!
    The avenging sword unsheathe;
    March on! march on! all hearts resolved
    On victory or death.

Now, now the dangerous storm is rolling,
    Which treacherous kings, confederate, raise;
The dogs of war, let loose, are howling,
    And lo! our fields and cities blaze;
And shall we basely view the ruin,
    While lawless force, with guilty stride,
    Spreads desolation far and wide,
With crimes and blood his hands imbruing?

With luxury and pride surrounded,
    The vile, insatiate despots dare,
Their thirst of power and gold unbounded,
    To meet and vend the light and air;
Like beasts of burden would they load us,
    Like gods would bid their slaves adore:
    But man is man, and who is more?
Then, shall they longer lash and goad us?

O Liberty! can man resign thee,
   Once having felt thy generous flame?
Can dungeons, bolts, or bars confine thee?
   Or whips thy noble spirit tame?
Too long the world has wept, bewailing
   That falsehood's dagger tyrants wield,
   But freedom is our sword and shield,
And all their arts are unavailing.
   To arms! to arms, ye brave!
   The avenging sword unsheathe;
   March on! march on! all hearts resolved
On victory or death.

Adapted from the French of Rouget de Lisle

Germany

The land where man evolves the impossible from his inner consciousness, where language bristles with consonants, and steins are foaming with beer; where efficiency is a creed and "Deutschland Ueber Alles" rivals the ten commandments; renowned for its Beethoven and Bismarck, Goethe and Schiller, its castles on the Rhine, and the Cologne masterpiece of Gothic art; famous for a military aristocracy and a Kaiser without a kingdom; withal a land of homely comfort, of kaffee-klatches, and food early and often; a land of mighty trenchermen where youth is dreaming of a new civilization and listening to Wagnerian strains.

DRACHENFELS

The castled crag of Drachenfels
Frowns o'er the wide and winding Rhine,
Whose breast of waters broadly swells
Between the banks which bear the vine,
And hills all rich with blossomed trees,
And fields which promise corn and wine,
And scattered cities crowning these,
Whose far white walls along them shine,
Have strewed a scene, which I should see
With double joy wert *thou* with me.

And peasant girls, with deep blue eyes,
And hands which offer early flowers,
Walk smiling o'er this paradise;
Above, the frequent feudal towers
Through green leaves lift their walls of gray,
And many a rock which steeply lowers,
And noble arch in proud decay,
Look o'er this vale of vintage-bowers;
But one thing want these banks of Rhine,—
Thy gentle hand to clasp in mine!

I send the lilies given to me;
Though long before thy hand they touch,
I know that they must withered be,
But yet reject them not as such;
For I have cherished them as dear,
Because they yet may meet thine eye,
And guide thy soul to mine even here,
When thou behold'st them drooping nigh,
And know'st them gathered by the Rhine,
And offered from my heart to thine!

The river nobly foams and flows,
The charm of this enchanted ground,
And all its thousand turns disclose
Some fresher beauty varying round:
The haughtiest breast its wish might bound
Through life to dwell delighted here;
Nor could on earth a spot be found
To nature and to me so dear,
Could thy dear eyes in following mine
Still sweeten more these banks of Rhine!

Lord Byron

THE LORELEI

Yonder we see it from the steamer's deck,
The haunted Mountain of the Lorelei—
The hanging crags sharp-cut against a sky
Clear as a sapphire without flaw or fleck.
'Twas here the Siren lay in wait to wreck
The fisher-lad.   At dusk, as he rowed by,
Perchance he heard her tender amorous cry,
And, seeing the wondrous whiteness of her neck,
Perchance would halt, and lean towards the shore;
Then she by that soft magic which she had
Would lure him, and in gossamers of her hair,
Gold upon gold, would wrap him o'er and o'er,
Wrap him, and sing to him, and drive him mad,
Then drag him down to no man knoweth where.

Thomas Bailey Aldrich

BINGEN ON THE RHINE

A soldier of the Legion lay dying in Algiers,
There was lack of woman's nursing, there was dearth of
    woman's tears;
But a comrade stood beside him, while his life-blood ebbed
    away,
And bent, with pitying glances, to hear what he might say.
The dying soldier faltered, as he took that comrade's
    hand,
And he said, "I nevermore shall see my own, my native land;
Take a message, and a token, to some distant friends of mine,
For I was born at Bingen,—at Bingen on the Rhine.

"Tell my brothers and companions, when they meet and
    crowd around,
To hear my mournful story, in the pleasant vineyard
    ground,
That we fought the battle bravely, and when the day was
    done,
Full many a corpse lay ghastly pale beneath the setting sun:
And, 'mid the dead and dying, were some grown old in
    wars,—
The death-wound on their gallant breasts, the last of many
    scars;
And some were young, and suddenly beheld life's morn
    decline,—
And one had come from Bingen,—fair Bingen on the
    Rhine.

"Tell my mother that her other sons shall comfort her old
    age;
For I was aye a truant bird, that thought his home a cage;

For my father was a soldier, and even as a child
My heart leaped forth to hear him tell of struggles fierce
    and wild;
And when he died, and left us to divide his scanty hoard,
I let them take whate'er they would,—but kept my father's
    sword;
And with boyish love I hung it where the bright light used
    to shine,
On the cottage wall at Bingen,—calm Bingen on the
    Rhine.

"Tell my sister not to weep for me, and sob with drooping
    head,
When the troops come marching home again with glad and
    and gallant tread,
But to look upon them proudly, with a calm and steadfast
    eye,
For her brother was a soldier too, and not afraid to die;
And if a comrade seek her love, I ask her in my name
To listen to him kindly, without regret or shame,
And to hang the old sword in its place (my father's sword
    and mine),
For the honor of old Bingen—dear Bingen on the Rhine.

"There's another,—not a sister; in the happy days gone by
You'd have known her by the merriment that sparkled in
    her eye;
Too innocent for coquetry,—too fond for idle scorning,—
O friend! I fear the lightest heart makes sometimes heav-
    iest mourning!
Tell her the last night of my life (for, ere the moon be
    risen,
My body will be out of pain, my soul be out of prison),—

I dreamed I stood with *her,* and saw the yellow sunlight shine
On the vine-clad hills of Bingen,—fair Bingen on the Rhine.

"I saw the blue Rhine sweep along,—I heard, or seemed to hear,
The German songs we used to sing, in chorus sweet and clear;
And down the pleasant river, and up the slanting hill,
The echoing chorus sounded, through the evening calm and still;
And her glad blue eyes were on me, as we passed, with friendly talk,
Down many a path beloved of yore, and well-remembered walk,
And her little hand lay lightly, confidingly in mine,—
But we'll meet no more at Bingen,—loved Bingen on the Rhine."

His trembling voice grew faint and hoarse,—his grasp was childish weak,—
His eyes put on a dying look,—he sighed and ceased to speak;
His comrade bent to lift him, but the spark of life had fled,—
The soldier of the Legion in a foreign land was dead!
And the soft moon rose up slowly, and calmly she looked down
On the red sand of the battle-field, with bloody corpses strown;
Yes, calmly on that dreadful scene her pale light seemed to shine,
As it shone on distant Bingen,—fair Bingen on the Rhine.

Caroline Elizabeth Norton

HEINE

Hartz Mountains

See! in the May afternoon,
O'er the fresh short turf of the Hartz,
A youth, with the foot of youth,
Heine! thou climbest again.
Up, through the tall dark firs
Warming their heads in the sun,
Checkering the grass with their shade,—
Up, by the stream with its huge
Moss-hung boulders and thin
Musical water half hid,—
Up, o'er the rock-strewn slope,
With the sinking sun, and the air
Chill, and shadows now
Long on the gray hillside,—
To the stone-roofed hut at the top.
Or, yet later, in watch
On the roof of the Brocken tower
Thou standest, gazing! to see
The broad red sun over field,
Forest and city and spire,
And mist-tracked stream of the wide,
Wide German land, going down
In a bank of vapors,—again
Standest! at nightfall, alone.

Or, next morning, with limbs
Rested by slumber, and heart
Freshened and light with the May,
O'er the gracious spurs coming down
Of the Lower Hartz, among oaks,

And beechen coverts, and copse
Of hazels green in whose depth
Ilse, the fairy transformed,
In a thousand water-breaks light
Pours her petulant youth,
Climbing the rock which juts
O'er the valley, the dizzily perched
Rock! to its Iron Cross
Once more thou cling'st; to the Cross
Clingest! with smiles, with a sigh.
Goethe, too, had been there.
In the long-past winter he came
To the frozen Hartz, with his soul
Passionate, eager, his youth
All in ferment;—but he
Destined to work and to live
Left it, and thou, alas!
Only to laugh and to die.

Matthew Arnold

NUREMBERG

In the valley of the Pegnitz, where across broad meadow-
    lands
Rise the blue Franconian mountains, Nuremberg, the
    ancient, stands.

Quaint old town of toil and traffic, quaint old town of art
    and song,
Memories haunt thy pointed gables, like the rooks that
    round them throng:

Memories of the Middle Ages, when the emperors, rough
    and bold,
Had their dwelling in thy castle, time-defying, centuries old;

And thy brave and thrifty burghers boasted, in their uncouth
    rhyme,
That their great imperial city stretched its hand through
    every clime.

In the court-yard of the castle, bound with many an iron
    band,
Stands the mighty linden planted by Queen Cunigunde's
    hand;

On the square, the oriel window, where in old heroic days
Sat the poet Melchior singing Kaiser Maximilian's praise.

Everywhere I see around me rise the wondrous world of
    Art:
Fountains wrought with richest sculpture standing in the
    common mart;

And above cathedral doorways saints and bishops carved in
stone,
By a former age commissioned as apostles to our own.

In the church of sainted Sebald sleeps enshrined his holy
dust,
And in bronze the Twelve Apostles guard from age to age
their trust;

In the church of sainted Lawrence stands a pix of sculp-
ture rare,
Like the foamy sheaf of fountains, rising through the painted
air.

Here, when Art was still religion, with a simple, reverent
heart,
Lived and labored Albrecht Dürer, the Evangelist of Art;

Hence in silence and in sorrow, toiling still with busy hand,
Like an emigrant he wandered, seeking for the Better Land.

Emigravit is the inscription on the tombstone where he lies;
Dead he is not, but departed,—for the artist never dies.

Fairer seems the ancient city, and the sunshine seems more
fair,
That he once has trod its pavement, that he once has
breathed its air!

Through these streets so broad and stately, these obscure
and dismal lanes,
Walked of yore the Meistersingers, chanting rude poetic
strains.

From remote and sunless suburbs came they to the friendly
    guild,
Building nests in Fame's great temple, as in spouts the swal-
    lows build.

As the weaver plied the shuttle, wove he too the mystic
    rhyme,
And the smith his iron measures hammered to the anvil's
    chime;

Thanking God, whose boundless wisdom makes the flowers
    of poesy bloom
In the forge's dust and cinders, in the tissues of the loom.

Here Hans Sachs, the cobbler-poet, laureate of the gentle
    craft,
Wisest of the Twelve Wise Masters, in huge folios sang
    and laughed.

But his house is now an alehouse, with a nicely sanded
    floor,
And a garland in the window, and his face above the door,

Painted by some humble artist, as in Adam Puschman's song,
As the old man gray and dovelike, with his great beard white
    and long.

And at night the swart mechanic comes to drown his cark
    and care,
Quaffing ale from pewter tankards, in the master's antique
    chair.

Vanished is the ancient splendor, and before my dreamy eye
Wave these mingled shapes and figures, like a faded tapestry.

Not thy Councils, not thy Kaisers, win for thee the world's
regard,
But thy painter, Albrecht Dürer, and Hans Sachs, thy cob-
bler-bard.

Thus, O Nuremberg, a wanderer from a region far away,
As he paced thy streets and court-yards, sang in thought his
careless lay:

Gathering from the pavement's crevice, as a floweret of the
soil,
The nobility of labor,—the long pedigree of toil.

Henry Wadsworth Longfellow

COLOGNE

In Kohln, a town of monks and bones
And pavements fang'd with murderous stones,
And rags, and hags, and hideous wenches;
I counted two and seventy stenches
All well-defined, and several stinks!
Ye Nymphs that reign o'er sewers and sinks,
The river Rhine, it is well known,
Doth wash your city of Cologne;
But tell me, Nymphs! what power divine
Shall henceforth wash the river Rhine?

Samuel T. Coleridge

DRESDEN

At Dresden on the Elbe, that handsome city
Where straw hats, verses and cigars are made,
They've built (it well may make us feel afraid),
A music club and music warehouse pretty.

Heinrich Heine

From: "Book of Songs, Sonnets, Dresden Poetry"

NATIONAL AIR

GERMANY

The Watch on the Rhine

A voice resounds like thunder-peal,
'Mid clashing waves and clang of steel:—
"The Rhine, the Rhine, the German Rhine!
Who guards to-day my stream divine?"

Chorus—Dear Fatherland, no danger thine:
       Firm stand thy sons to watch the Rhine!

They stand a hundred thousand strong,
Quick to avenge their country's wrong;
With filial love their bosoms swell,
They'll guard the sacred landmark well!

The dead of a heroic race
From heaven look down and meet their gaze;
They swear with dauntless heart, "O Rhine,
Be German as this breast of mine!

"While flows one drop of German blood,
Or sword remains to guard thy flood,
While rifle rests in patriot hand,—
No foe shall tread thy sacred strand!

"Our oath resounds, the river flows,
In golden light our banner glows;
Our hearts will guard thy stream divine:
The Rhine, the Rhine, the German Rhine!"

After the German of Max Schneckenburger

Switzerland

The synonym of scenic beauty, a perfect republic, though a pocket edition; the land of Mont Blanc, the snowy Jungfrau, the stern Matterhorn, and of the winter sports of Saint Moritz; the land of good inns, of the mythical William Tell, of Calvin and of Zwingli, and the birthplace of the League of Nations; whose symbol of frugal comfort, of constant industry and of happy contentment is the little chalet perched on her mountain sides.

AN ALPINE PICTURE

Stand here and look, and softly draw your breath
Lest the dread avalanche come crashing down!
How many leagues away is yonder town
Set flower-wise in the valley?   Far beneath
Our feet lies summer; here a realm of death,
Where never flower has blossomed nor bird flown.
The ancient water-courses are all strown
With drifts of snow, fantastic wreath on wreath;
And peak on peak against the stainless blue
The Alps like towering campanili stand,
Wondrous, with pinnacles of frozen rain,
Silvery, crystal, like the prism in hue.
O tell me, love, if this be Switzerland—
Or is it but the frost-work on the pane?

Thomas Bailey Aldrich

WILLIAM TELL

Chains may subdue the feeble spirit, but thee,
Tell, of the iron heart, they could not tame;
For thou wert of the mountains; they proclaim
The everlasting creed is written on the untrampled snow,
Thundered by torrents which no power can hold,
Save that of God, when he sends forth his cold,
And breathed by winds that through the free heavens blow.
Thou, while thy prison walls were dark around
Didst meditate the lesson Nature taught,
And to thy brief captivity was brought
A vision of thy Switzerland unbound.
The bitter cup they mingled strengthened thee
For the great work to set thy country free.

William Cullen Bryant

SONNET ON CHILLON

Eternal spirit of the chainless Mind!
Brightest in dungeons, Liberty! thou art,
For there thy habitation is the heart—
The heart which love of thee alone can bind;
And when thy sons to fetters are consign'd—
To fetters and the damp vault's dayless gloom,
Their country conquers with their martyrdom
And Freedom's fame finds wings on every wind.
Chillon! thy prison is a holy place
And thy sad floor an altar—for 'twas trod,
Until his very steps have left a trace
Worn, as if thy cold pavement were a sod,
By Bonnivard!   May none those marks efface!
For they appeal from tyranny to God.

Lord Byron

Italy

Here Caesar ruled and Cicero flamed into eloquence, and Dante dreamed, and Giotto built and Raphael painted; and here a freckled faced Genoan boy saw far out in the west a new world waiting for him; land of a menacing Etna, and of a blue Mediterranean, of olive groves and softly moving gondolas; land where the spirit of the legionnaires is abroad again, embodied in Mussolini, who dreams of a new Italy rising on the ruins of a mighty past; from whose gracious shores come the ravioli, spaghetti, chianti and the world's most beautiful potteries, and on whose Appian Way walk the ghosts of Roman statesmen, warriors and Christian martyrs.

TO ITALY

October, 1918

Fair land of dear desire,
  Where Beauty like a gleam
Has waked the hidden fire
  Of what our souls would dream!

Where shining ilex glistens,
  And cypress' sombre shade
Above dim fountains listens
  In some forgotten glade.

Oh! land of dear desire,
  Thy beauty sweeps again
My heart with sudden fire
  And burns away its pain.

I dream with Perugino
  On some far Umbrian hill,
Or pray with sweet St. Francis
  Till this world's fret is still.

Until my soul reposes
  As once, unscourged he lay,
Amid the thornless roses
  Until the break of day.

Dear Saint, who was the brother
  Of every living thing,
Could we to one another
  Thy gracious message bring,

The world renewed, awaking,
  Would shed the shattered, torn,
Grim night of its own making,
  And pledge a peace reborn.

Fair land of dear desire,
  Thy beauty like a gleam
Shall kindle and inspire
  What all our souls would dream!

Corinne Roosevelt Robinson

THE BRIDE OF ABYDOS

Canto I

Know ye the land where the cypress and myrtle
  Are emblems of deeds that are done in their clime,
Where the rage of the vulture, the love of the turtle,
  Now melt into sorrow, now madden to crime.

Lord Byron

GRAVE OF KEATS

Peace, peace! he is not dead, he doth not sleep
   He hath awakened from the dream of life—
'Tis we, who, lost in stormy visions, keep
    With phantoms an unprofitable strife,
    And in mad trance strike with our spirit's knife
Invulnerable nothings. We decay
   Like corpses in a charnel; fear and grief
Convulse us and consume us day by day,
And cold hopes swarm like worms within our living
    clay.

He has outsoared the shadow of our night;
   Envy and calumny, and hate and pain,
And that unrest which men miscall delight,
    Can touch him not and torture not again;
    From the contagion of the world's slow stain
He is secure, and now can never mourn
   A heart grown cold, a head grown gray in vain;
Nor, when the spirit's self has ceased to burn,
With sparkless ashes load an unlamented urn.

He lives, he wakes—'tis Death is dead, not he;
   Mourn not for Adonais.—Thou young Dawn,
Turn all thy dew to splendor, for from thee
    The spirit thou lamentest is not gone;
    Ye caverns and ye forests, cease to moan!
Cease, ye faint flowers and fountains, and thou Air,
   Which like a mourning veil thy scarf hadst thrown
O'er the abandoned Earth, now leave it bare
Even to the joyous stars which smile on its despair!

He is made one with Nature: there is heard
  His voice in all her music, from the moan
Of thunder to the song of night's sweet bird;
  He is a presence to be felt and known
  In darkness and in light, from herb and stone,
Spreading itself where'er that Power may move
  Which has withdrawn his being to his own;
Which wields the world with never-wearied love,
Sustains it from beneath, and kindles it above.

                          Percy Bysshe Shelley

SHELLEY'S SKYLARK

The Neighbourhood of Leghorn: March, 1887

Somewhere afield here something lies
    In Earth's oblivious eyeless trust
That moved a poet to prophecies—
    A pinch of unseen, unguarded dust:

The dust of the lark that Shelley heard,
    And made immortal through times to be;—
Though it only lived like another bird,
    And knew its immortality:

Lived its meek life; then, one day, fell—
    A little ball of feather and bone;
And how it perished, when piped farewell,
    And where it wastes, are alike unknown.

Maybe it rests in the loam I view,
    Maybe it throbs in the myrtle's green,
Maybe it sleeps in the coming hue
    Of a grape on the slopes of yon inland scene.

Go find it, faeries, go and find
    That tiny pinch of priceless dust,
And bring a casket silver-lined,
    And framed of gold that gems encrust;

And we will lay it safe therein,
    And consecrate it to endless time;
For it inspired a bard to win
    Ecstatic heights in thought and rhyme.

Thomas Hardy

[180]

VALLOMBROSA

And Vallombrosa, we two went to see
    Last June, beloved companion,—where sublime
The mountains live in holy families,
    And the slow pine-woods ever climb and climb
Half up their breasts; just stagger as they seize
    Some gray crag,—drop back with it many a time,
And straggle blindly down the precipice!
    The Vallombrosan brooks were strewn as thick
That June day, knee-deep, with dead beechen leaves,
    As Milton saw them ere his heart grew sick,
And his eyes blind. I think the monks and beeves
    Are all the same too: scarce they have changed the wick
On good Saint Gualbert's altar; which receives
    The convent's pilgrims; and the pool in front
Wherein the hill-stream trout are cast, to wait
    The beatific vision, and the grunt
Used at refectory, keeps its weedy state,
    To baffle saintly abbots, who would count
The fish across their breviary, nor 'bate
    The measure of their steps. O waterfalls
And forests! sound and silence! mountains bare,
    That leap up, peak by peak, and catch the palls
Of purple and silver mist, to rend and share
    With one another, at electric calls
Of life in the sunbeams,—till we cannot dare
    Fix your shapes, learn your number! we must think
Your beauty and your glory helped to fill
    The cup of Milton's soul so to the brink,
That he no more was thirsty when God's will
    Had shattered to his sense the last chain-link
By which he drew from Nature's visible
    The fresh well-water. Satisfied by this,

He sang of Adam's Paradise and smiled,
  Remembering Vallombrosa. Therefore is
The place divine to English man and child;—
  We all love Italy.

Elizabeth Barrett Browning

PETRARCH'S TOMB

There is a tomb in Arqua;—reared in air,
Pillared in their sarcophagus, repose
The bones of Laura's lover; here repair
Many familiar with his well-sung woes,
The pilgrims of his genius. He arose
To raise a language, and his land reclaim
From the dull yoke of her barbaric foes;
Watering the tree which bears his lady's name
With his melodious tears, he gave himself to fame.

They kept his dust in Arqua, where he died;
The mountain-village where his latter days
Went down the vale of years; and 'tis their pride,—
An honest pride,—and let it be their praise,
To offer to the passing stranger's gaze
His mansion and his sepulchre; both plain
And venerably simple, such as raise
A feeling more accordant with his strain
Than if a pyramid formed his monumental fane.

Lord Byron

BY THE ARNO

The oleander on the wall
Grows crimson in the dawning light,
Though the grey shadows of the night
Lie yet on Florence like a pall.

The dew is bright upon the hill
And bright the blossoms overhead,
But ah! the grasshoppers have fled,
The little, Attic song is still.

Only the leaves are gently stirred
By the soft breathing of the gale,
And in the almond-scented vale
The lonely nightingale is heard.

The day will make thee silent soon
O nightingale, sing on for love!
While yet upon the shadowy grove
Splinter the arrows of the moon.

Before across the silent lawn
In sea-green mist the morning steals,
And to love's frightened eyes reveals
The long white fingers of the dawn

Fast climbing up the eastern sky
To grasp and slay the shuddering night,
All careless of my heart's delight,
Or if the nightingale should die.

Oscar Wilde.

WRITTEN AT FLORENCE

O world, in very truth thou art too young;
When wilt thou learn to wear the garb of age?
World, with thy covering of yellow flowers,
Hast thou forgot what generations sprung
Out of thy loins and loved thee and are gone?
Hast thou no place in all their heritage
Where thou dost only weep, that I may come
Nor fear the mockery of thy yellow flowers?

   O world, in very truth thou art too young.
The heroic wealth of passionate emprize
Built thee fair cities for thy naked plains:
How hast thou set thy summer growth among
The broken stones which were their palaces!
Hast thou forgot the darkness where *he* lies
Who made thee beautiful, or have thy bees
Found out his grave to build their honeycombs?

O world, in very truth thou art too young:
They gave thee love who measured out thy skies,
And, when they found for thee another star,
Who made a festival and straightway hung
The jewel on thy neck. O merry world,
Hast thou forgot the glory of those eyes
Which first look'd love in thine? Thou hast not
     furl'd
One banner of thy bridal car for them.

   O world, in very truth thou art too young.
There was a voice which sang about thy spring,
Till winter froze the sweetness of his lips,
And lo, the worms had hardly left his tongue

[185]

Before thy nightingales were come again.
O world, what courage hast thou thus to sing?
Say, has thy merriment no secret pain,
No sudden weariness that thou art young?

Wilfrid Scawen Blunt

THE OLD BRIDGE AT FLORENCE

Taddeo Gaddi built me. I am old,
Five centuries old. I plant my foot of stone
Upon the Arno, as St. Michael's own
Was planted on the dragon. Fold by fold
Beneath me as it struggles, I behold
Its glistening scales. Twice hath it overthrown
My kindred and companions. Me alone
It moveth not, but is by me controlled.
I can remember when the Medici
Were driven from Florence; longer still ago
The final wars of Ghibelline and Guelf.
Florence adorns me with her jewelry;
And when I think that Michael Angelo
Hath leaned on me, I glory in myself.

Henry Wadsworth Longfellow

BEATA BEATRIX

"Ella ha perduta la sua Beatrice:
E le parole ch'uom di lei puo dire
Hanno virtu di far piangere altrui."
Vita Nuova.

And was it thine, the light whose radiance shed
   Love's halo round the gloom of Dante's brow?
   Was thine the hand that touched his hand, and thou
   The spirit to his inmost spirit wed?
O gentle, O most pure, what shall be said
   In praise of these to whom Love's minstrels bow?
   O heart that held his heart, for ever now
   Thou with his glory shalt be garlanded.
Lo, 'mid the twilight of the waning years,
   Firenze claims once more our love, our tears:
   But thou, triumphant on the throne of song,—
By Mary seated in the realm above,—
   O give us of that gift than death more strong,
   The loving spirit that won Dante's love.

Samuel Waddington

DRIFTING

My soul to-day
Is far away,
Sailing the Vesuvian Bay;
My wingèd boat,
A bird afloat,
Swings round the purple peaks remote:—

Round purple peaks
It sails and seeks
Blue inlets and their crystal creeks,
Where high rocks throw,
Through deeps below,
A duplicated golden glow.

Far, vague and dim,
The mountains swim;
While on Vesuvius' misty brim,
With outstretched hands,
The gray smoke stands
O'erlooking the volcanic lands.

Here Ischia smiles
O'er liquid miles;
And yonder, bluest of the isles,
Calm Capri waits,
Her sapphire gates
Beguiling to her bright estates.

I heed not, if
My rippling skiff
Float swift or slow from cliff to cliff;
With dreamful eyes
My spirit lies
Under the walls of Paradise.

Under the walls
Where swells and falls
The Bay's deep breast at intervals,
At peace I lie,
Blown softly by
A cloud upon this liquid sky.

The day, so mild,
Is Heaven's own child,
With Earth and Ocean reconciled;
The airs I feel
Around me steal
Are murmuring to the murmuring keel.

Over the rail
My hand I trail
Within the shadow of the sail,
A joy intense,
The cooling sense
Glides down my drowsy indolence.

With dreamful eyes
My spirit lies
Where Summer sings and never dies,—
O'erveiled with vines
She glows and shines
Among her future oil and wines.

Her children, hid
The cliffs amid,
Are gamboling with the gamboling kid;
Or down the walls
With tipsy calls,
Laugh on the rocks like waterfalls.

The fisher's child,
With tresses wild,
Unto the smooth, bright sand beguiled,
With glowing lips
Sings as she skips,
Or gazes at the far-off ships.

Yon deep bark goes
Where traffic blows,
From lands of sun to lands of snows;—
This happier one,
Its course is run
From lands of snow to lands of sun.

O happy ship,
To rise and dip,
With the blue crystal at your lip!
O happy crew,
My heart with you
Sails, and sails, and sings anew!

No more, no more
The worldly shore
Upbraids me with its loud uproar!
With dreamful eyes
My spirit lies
Under the walls of Paradise!

Thomas Buchanan Read

SELECTION FROM DIPSYCHUS

In a Gondola

Afloat; we move! Delicious! Ah,
What else is like the gondola?
This level floor of liquid glass
Begins beneath us swift to pass,
It goes as though it went alone
By some impulsion of its own.
(How light it moves, how softly! Ah,
Were all things like the gondola!)

How light it moves, how softly! Ah,
Could life as does our gondola
Unvexed with quarrels, aims and cares,
And moral duties and affairs,
Unswaying, noiseless, swift and strong,
For ever thus—thus glide along
(How light we move, how softly! Ah
Were life but as the gondola!)

With no more motion than should bear
A languid freshness on the air;
With no more effort than expressed
The need and naturalness of rest,
Which we beneath a grateful shade
Should take on peaceful pillows laid!
(How light we move, how softly! Ah,
Were life but as the gondola!)

In one unbroken passage borne
To closing night or opening morn

Uplift at whiles slow eyes to mark
Some palace front, some passing bark;
Through windows catch the varying shore,
And hear the soft turns of the oar.
(How light we move, how softly! Ah,
Were life but as the gondola!)

How light we go, how soft we skim
And all in moonlight seems to swim!
In moonlight is it now, or shade?
In planes of sure divisions made,
By angles sharp of palace walls
The clear light and the shadow falls,
(How light we go, how softly! Ah,
Life should be as the gondola!)

Arthur Hugh Clough

ON THE EXTINCTION OF THE VENETIAN
REPUBLIC, 1802

Once did she hold the gorgeous East in fee;
   And was the safeguard of the West: the worth
Of Venice did not fall below her birth,
Venice, the eldest Child of Liberty.
She was a maiden City, bright and free;
   No guile seduced, no force could violate;
   And, when she took unto herself a mate,
She must espouse the everlasting Sea.
And what if she had seen those glories fade,
   Those titles vanish, and that strength decay;
Yet shall some tribute of regret be paid
   When her long life hath reach'd its final day:
Men are we, and must grieve when even the Shade
   Of that which once was great is pass'd away.

William Wordsworth

SICILY

The Song of Callicles

Through the black, rushing smoke-bursts,
  Thick breaks the red flame.
All Etna heaves fiercely
  Her forest-clothed frame.

Not here, O Apollo!
  Are haunts meet for thee.
But where Helicon breaks down
  In cliff to the sea.

Where the moon-silver'd inlets
  Send far their light voice
Up the still vale of Thisbe,
  O speed, and rejoice!

On the sward at the cliff-top,
  Lie strewn the white flocks;
On the cliff-side, the pigeons
  Roost deep in the rocks.

In the moonlight the shepherds,
  Soft lull'd by the rills,
Lie wrapt in their blankets,
  Asleep on the hills.

—What forms are these coming
  So white through the gloom?
What garments out-glistening
  The gold-flower'd broom?

What sweet-breathing Presence
  Out-perfumes the thyme?

What voices enrapture
  The night's balmy prime? —

'Tis Apollo comes leading
  His choir, The Nine.
—The Leader is fairest,
  But all are divine.

They are lost in the hollows.
  They stream up again.
What seeks on this mountain
  The glorified train? —

They bathe on this mountain,
  In the spring by their road.
Then on to Olympus,
  Their endless abode.

—Whose praise do they mention:
  Of what is it told?—
What will be for ever.
  What was from of old.

First hymn they the Father
  Of all things: and then
The rest of Immortals,
  The action of men.

The Day in his hotness,
  The strife with the palm;
The Night in her silence,
  The Stars in their calm.

Matthew Arnold

IN A GONDOLA

The moth's kiss, first!
Kiss me as if you made me believe
You were not sure, this eve,
How my face, your flower, had pursed
Its petals up; so, here and there
You brush it, till I grow aware
Who wants me, and wide ope I burst.

The bee's kiss, now!
Kiss me as if you enter'd gay
My heart at some noonday,
A bud that dares not disallow
The claim, so all is render'd up,
And passively its shatter'd cup
Over your head to sleep I bow.

Robert Browning

VENICE

Venice, thou Siren of sea-cities, wrought
By mirage, built on water, stair o'er stair,
Of sunbeams and cloud-shadows, phantom-fair,
With naught of earth to mar thy sea-born thought!
Thou floating film upon the wonder-fraught
Ocean of dreams! Thou hast no dream so rare
As are thy sons and daughters, they who wear
Foam-flakes of charm from thine enchantment caught!
O dark brown eyes! O tangles of dark hair!
O heaven-blue eyes, blonde tresses where the breeze
Plays over sun-burned cheeks in sea-blown air!
Firm limbs of moulded bronze! frank debonair
Smiles of deep-bosomed women! Loves that seize
Man's soul, and waft her on storm-melodies!

John Addington Symonds

VENICE

White swan of cities slumbering in thy nest
So wonderfully built among the reeds
Of the lagoon that fences thee and feeds,
As sayeth the old historian and thy guest.

Henry Wadsworth Longfellow

From: "Venice"

VENICE

From "Childe Harold's Pilgrimage"

I stood in Venice on the Bridge of Sighs,
A palace and a prison on each hand:
I saw from out the wave her structures rise
As from the stroke of the enchanter's wand;
A thousand years their cloudy wings expand
Around me, and a dying Glory smiles
O'er the far times, when many a subject land
Looked to the wingèd Lion's marble piles,
Where Venice sate in state, throned on her hundred isles!

She looks a sea Cybele, fresh from ocean,
Rising with her tiara of proud towers
At airy distance, with majestic motion,
And such she was; her daughters had their dowers
From spoils of nations, and the exhaustless East
Poured in her lap all gems in sparkling showers:
In purple was she robed, and of her feast
Monarchs partook, and deemed their dignity increased.

In Venice Tasso's echoes are no more,
And silent rows the songless gondolier;
Her palaces are crumbling to the shore,
And music meets not always now the ear:
Those days are gone, but Beauty still is here;
States fall, arts fade, but Nature doth not die,
Nor yet forget how Venice once was dear,
The pleasant place of all festivity,
The revel of the earth, the masque of Italy!

But unto us she hath a spell beyond
Her name in story, and her long array
Of mighty shadows, whose dim forms despond
Above the Dogeless city's vanished sway:
Ours is a trophy which will not decay
With the Rialto; Shylock and the Moor,
And Pierre, cannot be swept or worn away,—
The keystones of the arch!—though all were o'er,
For us repeopled were the solitary shore.

Lord Byron

SAN MARCO'S BELLS

Amid dim frescoed cloisters rich
With faded saints and footworn tombs,
The soul-stress of those vanished monks
    Still looms.

Life upward, inward turned was full
Of spirit-stirrings, and they wrought
On altars, walls and manuscripts
    Their thought.

Here raptured Fra Angelico
In heaven's azure, flame, and gold,
Portrayed his radiant visitants
    Of old.

Here Benedetto's burnished chaunts
And gorgeous missals grew apace,
And gentle industries filled all
    The place.

Bartolommeo anguished here
And as he painted, kneeled in prayer—
Each prayer a vision, for his Lord
    Was there.

Savonarola pacing slow
The prophets pondered e'er he hurled
His mad anathemas against
    The world.

I wonder do they ofttimes steal
Unheeded to their lonely cells
In old San Marco when they hear
    Its bells.

Gertrude Huntington McGiffert

[202]

VENICE

A Fragment

'Tis midnight—but it is not dark
Within thy spacious place, Saint Mark!
The Lights within, the Lamps without,
Shine above the revel rout.
The brazen Steeds are glittering o'er
The holy building's massy door,
Glittering with their collars of gold,
The goodly work of the days of old—
And the winged Lion stern and solemn
Frowns from the height of his hoary column,
Facing the palace in which doth lodge
The ocean-city's dreaded Doge.
The palace is proud—but near it lies,
Divided by the "Bridge of Sighs,"
The dreary dwelling where the State
Enchains the captives of their hate:
These—they perish or they pine;
But which their doom may none divine:
Many have pass'd that Arch of pain,
But none retraced their steps again.

It is a princely colonnade!
And wrought around a princely place,
When that vast edifice display'd
Looks with its venerable face
Over the far and subject sea,
Which makes the fearless isles so free!
And 'tis a strange and noble pile,
Pillar'd into many an aisle:
Every pillar fair to see,
Marble—jasper—and porphyry—

The church of Saint Mark—which stands hard by
With fretted pinnacles on high,
And cupola and minaret;
More like the mosque of orient lands,
Than the fanes wherein we pray,
And Mary's blessed likeness stands.

Lord Byron

BARCAROLE

On the winding ways of Venice
Where there's little chance for tennis,
   But spumone, zabaione
      And chianti sweetly cheer,
Went a roving Yankee Doodler
(A canoedelling canoedler)
   With a shambling, gambling,
      Rambling, scrambling,
         Gondolling gondolier.

Past San Marco's gorgeous duomo
Where the local *genus homo*
   Works at guiding, thus providing
      For his wives and children dear,
Past the Palace of the Doges
With its loges and gamboges
   Rowed the shyly smiley,
      Highly wily,
         Gondolling gondolier.

Through the narrow canaletti
Where they hang the fresh spaghetti
   For the savor and the flavor
      Which pervade the atmosphere,
Through the redolent Rialto,
Singing tenor and contralto,
   Oared the chanting, ranting,
      Gallivanting,
         Gondolling gondolier.

Then across to view the Lido
Where the universal credo
  Is, "We need you and we bleed you
    And we're here because we're here,"
On the azure Adriatic
In his cockle-shell piratic
  Steered the dashing, plashing,
    Crimson-sashing,
      Gondolling gondolier.

At the hour when rising Luna
Silvers all the calm laguna,
  When the pasti and the asti
    On the festal board appear,
Where the gondole are stranded
Was the stranger safely landed
  By the daring, flaring,
    Earring-wearing,
      Gondolling gondolier.

"Give-a lire hundre'-twenty
For da trippa longa plenty!"
  In such argot to his cargo
    Spake that licensed buccaneer.
"Why, you darned Venetian boodler!"
Cried the wrathful Yankee Doodler
  To the overcharging,
    Fee-enlarging,
      Gondolling gondolier.

But the boatman swore, "Sapristi!
I go tella da Fascisti!"
  So the rover forked it over
    Using language quite severe

As he blustered, "Call me Dennis,
But I'll stay and warn all Venice
  Of the thieving, reaving,
    Arch-deceiving,
      Gondolling gondolier!"

So the Yankee, never flitting,
On the Molo still is sitting,
  Objurgating, comminating
    That aquatic profiteer,
Who inhales his vermicelli
Singing scandalous stornelli,
  Oh, the shameless, tameless,
    Fameless, nameless,
      Gondolling gondolier!

Arthur Guiterman

ROME

I am in Rome. Oft as the morning ray
Visits these eyes, waking at once I cry
Whence this excess of joy? What has befallen me?
And from within a thrilling voice replies,
"Thou art in Rome." A thousand busy thoughts
Rush on my mind, a thousand images;
And I spring up as girt to run a race.

Samuel Rogers

From: "Rome"

ITALIAN RHAPSODY

In tears I tossed my coin from Trevi's edge
A coin unsordid as a bond of love—
And, with the instinct of the homing dove
I gave to Rome my rendezvous and pledge.
And when imperious Death
Has quenched my flame of breath
Oh, let me join the faithful shades
That throng that fount above!

Robert U. Johnson

THE COLISEUM

Type of the antique Rome! Rich reliquary
Of lofty contemplation left to Time
By buried centuries of pomp and power!
At length—at length—after so many days
Of weary pilgrimage and burning thirst,
(Thirst for the springs of lore that in thee lie,)
I kneel, an altered and an humble man,
Amid thy shadows, and so drink within
My very soul thy grandeur, gloom, and glory!

Vastness! and Age! and Memories of Eld!
Silence! and Desolation! and dim Night!
I feel ye now—I feel ye in your strength—
O spells more sure than e'er Judæan king
Taught in the gardens of Gethsemane!
O charms more potent than the rapt Chaldee
Ever drew down from out the quiet stars!

Here, where a hero fell, a column falls!
Here, where the mimic eagle glared in gold,
A midnight vigil holds the swarthy bat!
Here, where the dames of Rome their gilded hair
Waved to the wind, now wave the reed and thistle!
Here, where on golden throne the monarch lolled,
Glides, spectre-like, unto his marble home,
Lit by the wan light of the hornèd moon,
The swift and silent lizard of the stones!

But stay! these walls—this crumbling frieze—
These shattered cornices—this wreck—this ruin—
These stones—alas! these gray stones—are they all—

All of the famed and the colossal left
By the corrosive Hours to Fate and me?

"Not all"—the Echoes answer me—"not all!
"Prophetic sounds and loud, arise forever
"From us, and from all Ruin, unto the wise,
"As melody from Memnon to the Sun.
"We rule the hearts of mightiest men—we rule
"With a despotic sway all giant minds.
"We are not impotent—we pallid stones.
"Not all our power is gone—not all our fame—
"Not all the magic of our high renown—
"Not all the wonder that encircles us—
"Not all the mysteries that in us lie—
"Not all the memories that hang upon
"And cling around about us as a garment,
"Clothing us in a robe of more than glory."

Edgar Allan Poe

THE FOUNTAIN OF TREVI

The Coliseum lifts at night
  Its broken cells more proudly far
Than in the noonday's naked light,
  For every rent enshrines a star:
  On Cæsar's hill the royal Lar
Presides within his mansion old:
  Decay and Death no longer mar
The moon's atoning mist of gold.

Still lingering near the shrines renewed,
  We sadly, fondly, look our last;
Each trace concealed of spoilage rude
  From old or late iconoclast,
  Till, Trajan's whispering forum passed,
We hear the waters, showering bright,
  Of Trevi's ancient fountain, cast
Their woven music on the night.

The Genius of the Tiber nods
  Benign, above his tilted urn:
Kneel down and drink! the beckoning gods
  This last libation will not spurn.
  Drink, and the old enchantment learn
That hovers yet o'er Trevi's foam—
  The promise of a sure return,
Fresh footsteps in the dust of Rome!

Kneel down and drink; the golden days
  Here lived and dreamed shall dawn again;
Albano's hill, through purple haze,
  Again shall crown the Latin plain.

Whatever stains of Time remain,
Left by the years that intervene,
  Lo! Trevi's fount shall toss its rain
To wash the pilgrim's forehead clean.

Drink, and depart! for Life is just;
  She gives to Faith a master-key
To ope the gates of dreams august,
  And take from joys in memory
  The certainty of joys to be;
And Trevi's basins shall be bare
  Ere we again shall fail to see
Their silver in the Roman air.

Bayard Taylor

SAINT PETER'S BY MOONLIGHT

Low hung the moon when first I stood in Rome;
Midway she seemed attracted from her sphere,
On those twin fountains shining broad and clear
Whose floods, not mindless of their mountain home,
Rise there in clouds of rainbow mist and foam.
That hour fulfilled the dream of many a year;
Through that thin mist, with joy akin to fear,
The steps I saw, the pillars, last, the dome.
A spiritual empire there embodied stood;
The Roman Church there met me face to face:
Ages, sealed up, of evil and of good
Slept in that circling colonnade's embrace.
Alone I stood, a stranger and alone,
Changed by that stony miracle to stone.

Sir Aubrey De Vere

THE CITY OF MY LOVE

She sits among the eternal hills,
  Their crown, thrice glorious and dear,
Her voice is as a thousand tongues
  Of silver fountains, gurgling clear;

Her breath is prayer, her life is love,
  And worship of all lovely things;
Her children have a gracious port,
  Her beggars show the blood of kings.

By old Tradition guarded close,
  None doubt the grandeur she has seen;
Upon her venerable front
  Is written: "I was born a Queen!"

She rules the age by Beauty's power,
  As once she ruled by armèd might;
The Southern sun doth treasure her
  Deep in his golden heart of light.

Awe strikes the traveller when he sees
  The vision of her distant dome,
And a strange spasm wrings his heart
  As the guide whispers, "There is Rome!"

Rome of the Romans! where the gods
  Of Greek Olympus long held sway;
Rome of the Christian, Peter's tomb,
  The Zion of our later day.

Rome, the mailed Virgin of the world,
  Defiance on her brows and breast;

Rome, to voluptuous pleasure won,
   Debauched, and locked in drunken rest.

Rome, in her intellectual day,
   Europe's intriguing step-dame grown,
Rome, bowed to weakness and decay,
   A canting, mass-frequenting crone.

Then the unlettered man plods on,
   Half chiding at the spell he feels,
The artist pauses at the gate,
   And on the wondrous threshold kneels.

The sick man lifts his languid head
   For those soft skies and balmy airs;
The pilgrim tries a quicker pace,
   And hugs remorse, and patters prayers.

For even the grass that feeds the herds
   Methinks some unknown virtue yields;
The very hinds in reverence tread
   The precincts of the ancient fields.

But wrapt in gloom of night and death,
   I crept to thee, dear mother Rome;
And in thy hospitable heart
   Found rest and comfort, health and home.

And friendships, warm and living still,
   Although their dearest joys are fled;
True sympathies, that bring to life
   That better self, so often dead.

For all the wonder that thou wert,
  For all the dear delight thou art,
Accept a homage from my lips,
  That warms again a wasted heart.

And, though it seem a childish prayer,
  I've breathed it oft, that when I die,
As thy remembrance dear in it,
  That heart in thee might buried lie.

                              Julia Ward Howe

POMPEIAN QUATRAIN

New Excavations

A workman with a spade in half a day
Can push two thousand lagging years away;
See, how the tragic villas, one by one,
Like lazy lizards creep into the sun.

Leonora Speyer

CAPRI

When beauty grows too great to bear
  How shall I ease me of its ache,
For beauty more than bitterness
  Makes the heart break.

Now while I watch the dreaming sea
  With isles like flowers against her breast,
Only one voice in all the world
  Could give me rest.

Sara Teasdale

NAPLES

Nisida and Prosida are laughing in the light,
Capri is a dewy flower lifting into sight,
Posilipo kneels and looks in the burnished sea,
Naples crowds her million roofs close as close can be;
Round about the mountain's crest a flag of smoke is hung—
Oh when God made Italy he was gay and young!

Sara Teasdale

NEAPOLITAN

Naples seems mostly mountains and mules,
and on a cloudy occasion,
mountains have the shade of mules,
donkeys the colour of mice.
Of all Neapolitan creatures,
donkeys alone never cease:
twinkling hoofs darting madly,
crazy carts hitched to their peace.
As mountains are sure not to move,
no matter what clouds may attempt,
the donkeys look further like mites
brushing endless high walls for escape.
When such queer mice venture so far—
forget they're born donkeys—
as to clatter right up sheer heights—
at right angles regardless of laws! —
their hoofs must have grown monkey paws!
and now should those simians clamber,
nay, scale tips of peaks themselves? —
don't be surprised any longer
if they should begin crawling skies!
Then one might readily ponder—
and still not offend their Creator—
there's nothing really left over
but to fancy them flies!

Alfred Kreymborg

ODE

The Mediterranean

Of thee the Northman by his beachèd galley
Dreamt, as he watched the never-setting Ursa
And longed for summer and thy light, O sacred
      Mediterranean.

Unseen he loved thee; for the heart within him
Knew earth had gardens where he might be blessed
Putting away long dreams and aimless, barbarous
      Hunger for battle.

The foretaste of thy languors thawed his bosom;
A great need drove him to thy caverned islands
From the gray, endless reaches of the outer
      Desert of ocean.

He saw thy pillars, saw thy sudden mountains
Wrinkled and stark, and in their crooked gorges,
'Neath peeping pine and cypress, guessed the torrent
      Smothered in flowers.

Thine incense to the sun, thy gathered vapours,
He saw suspended on the flanks of Taurus,
Or veiling the snowed bosom of the virgin
      Sister of Atlas.

He saw the luminous top of wide Olympus,
Fit for the happy gods; he saw the pilgrim
River, with rains of Ethiopia flooding
      Populous Egypt.

And having seen, he loved thee. His racked spirit,
By the breath tempered and the light that clothes thee,
Forgot the monstrous gods, and made of Nature
      Mistress and mother.

The more should I, O fatal sea, before thee
Of alien words make echoes to thy music;
For I was born where first the rills of Tagus
      Turn to the westward,

And wandering long, alas! have need of drinking
Deep of the patience of thy perfect sadness,
O thou that constant through the change of ages,
      Beautiful ever,

Never wast wholly young and void of sorrows,
Nor ever canst be old, while yet the morning
Kindles thy ripples, or the golden evening
      Dyes thee in purple.

Thee, willing to be tamed but still untamable,
The Roman called his own until he perished,
As now the busy English hover o'er thee,
      Stalwart and noble;

But all is naught to thee, while no harsh winter
Congeals thy fountains, and the blown Sahara
Chokes not with dreadful sand thy deep and placid
      Rock-guarded havens.

Thou carest not what men may tread thy margin;
Nor I, while from some heather-scented headland
I may behold thy beauty, the eternal
      Solace of mortals.

George Santayana

ITALY

Italy, my Italy,
Queen Mary's saying serves for me
(When fortune's malice lost her Calais)
Open my heart and you will see
Graved inside of it "Italy."

Robert Browning

From: "Men and Women"

NATIONAL AIR

To arms, men, to arms, men,
The graves loose their captives, arise our departed,
Our martyrs come forth, all our heroes great hearted,
With sabre in hand and their brows crowned with laurel,
The fame and the name of Italia their star!
Make haste, oh make haste, forward gallant battalions,
Fling out to the winds flags for all, ye Italians!
Rise all with your weapons, rise all fire impassioned,
Rise all fire impassioned, Italians ye are!
Depart from our homeland, depart, oh ye strangers,
This hour gives the signal, betake you afar.

The land famed for flowers, for poets, for singing
Once more be a land where the sword blows are ringing,
Our hands may be bound with a hundred harsh fetters,
But still they can brandish Legnano's bright swords.
The Austrian staff no Italian belabors;
The race born of Rome do not jest with their sabres;
No longer will Italy put up with her tyrants
Too many long years have we harbored their hordes.
Depart from our homelands, depart, oh ye strangers,
The hour gives the signal, betake you afar.

For us are the dwellings of Italy fashioned,
While yours on the Danube must henceforth be stationed.
You've ravaged our fields, yea our bread you have stolen.
Our sons for ourselves we desire to enroll.
The Alps with the two seas mark Italy's borders,
Our fire blazing chariots shall mow down the warders.

GARIBALDI'S WAR HYMN

All signs of the former frontier shall be cancelled
One banner alone let us raise o'er the whole.
Depart from our homeland, depart, oh ye strangers
This hour gives the signal, betake you afar.

Attributed to Olivieri

Greece

"*The mountains look on Marathon, and Marathon looks on the sea*"; home of Pericles and Phidias, of Plato and Praxiteles, of Alexander of Macedon who conquered a world, and of Aristotle his master, who was sovereign of the mind; the land of gods and goddesses who watched over the fate of man from their home on Mount Olympus; land of the Parthenon and of the city of Athens which gave to the world logic, philosophy, drama and art; land of golden sunshine and blue skies, of great athletes and beautiful women, and of a crown prince who married a tin-plate queen.

THE ISLES OF GREECE

The isles of Greece! the isles of Greece!
  Where burning Sappho loved and sung,
Where grew the arts of war and peace,
  Where Delos rose, and Phœbus sprung!
Eternal summer gilds them yet,
But all, except their sun, is set.

The Scian and the Teian muse,
  The hero's harp, the lover's lute,
Have found the fame your shores refuse:
  Their place of birth alone is mute
To sounds which echo further west
Than your sires' Islands of the Blest.

The mountains look on Marathon—
  And Marathon looks on the sea;
And musing there an hour alone,
  I dream'd that Greece might still be free;
For standing on the Persians' grave,
I could not deem myself a slave.

A king sate on the rocky brow
  Which looks o'er sea-born Salamis;
And ships, by thousands, lay below,
  And men in nations;—all were his!
He counted them at break of day—
  And when the sun set, where were they?

And where are they? and where art thou,
  My country? On thy voiceless shore

The heroic lay is tuneless now—
    The heroic bosom beats no more!
And must thy lyre, so long divine,
Degenerate into hands like mine?

'Tis something in the dearth of fame,
    Though link'd among a fetter'd race,
To feel at least a patriot's shame,
    Even as I sing, suffuse my face;
For what is left the poet here?
For Greeks a blush—for Greece a tear.

Must *we* but weep o'er days more blest?
    Must *we* but blush?—Our fathers bled.
Earth! render back from out thy breast
    A remnant of our Spartan dead!
Of the three hundred grant but three,
To make a new Thermopylæ!

What, silent still? and silent all?
    Ah! no;—the voices of the dead
Sound like a distant torrent's fall,
    And answer, 'Let one living head,
But one, arise,—we come, we come!'
'Tis but the living who are dumb.

In vain—in vain: strike other chords;
    Fill high the cup with Samian wine!
Leave battles to the Turkish hordes,
    And shed the blood of Scio's vine!
Hark! rising to the ignoble call—
How answers each bold Bacchanal!

You have the Pyrrhic dance as yet;
    Where is the Pyrrhic phalanx gone?
Of two such lessons, why forget
    The nobler and the manlier one?
You have the letters Cadmus gave—
Think ye he meant them for a slave?

Fill high the bowl with Samian wine!
    We will not think of themes like these!
It made Anacreon's song divine:
    He served—but served Polycrates—
A tyrant; but our masters then
Were still, at least, our countrymen.

The tyrant of the Chersonese
    Was freedom's best and bravest friend;
That tyrant was Miltiades!
    O that the present hour would lend
Another despot of the kind!
Such chains as his were sure to bind.

Fill high the bowl with Samian wine!
    On Suli's rock, and Parga's shore,
Exists the remnant of a line
    Such as the Doric mothers bore;
And there, perhaps, some seed is sown,
The Heracleidan blood might own.

Trust not for freedom to the Franks—
    They have a king who buys and sells;
In native swords and native ranks
    The only hope of courage dwells:
But Turkish force and Latin fraud
Would break your shield, however broad.

Fill high the bowl with Samian wine!
  Our virgins dance beneath the shade—
I see their glorious black eyes shine;
  But gazing on each glowing maid,
My own the burning tear-drop laves,
To think such breasts must suckle slaves.

Place me on Sunium's marbled steep,
  Where nothing, save the waves and I,
May hear our mutual murmurs sweep;
  There, swan-like, let me sing and die:
A land of slaves shall ne'er be mine—
Dash down yon cup of Samian wine!

Lord Byron

ODE ON A GRECIAN URN

Thou still unravish'd bride of quietness,
  Thou foster-child of Silence and slow Time,
Sylvan historian, who canst thus express
  A flowery tale more sweetly than our rhyme:
What leaf-fringed legend haunts about thy shape
  Of deities or mortals, or of both,
    In Tempe or the dales of Arcady?
  What men or gods are these? What maidens loth?
What mad pursuit? What struggle to escape?
  What pipes and timbrels? What wild ecstasy?

Heard melodies are sweet, but those unheard
  Are sweeter; therefore, ye soft pipes, play on;
Not to the sensual ear, but, more endear'd
  Pipe to the spirit ditties of no tone:
Fair youth, beneath the trees, thou canst not leave
  Thy song, nor ever can those trees be bare;
    Bold Lover, never, never canst thou kiss,
Though winning near the goal,—yet, do not grieve;
  She cannot fade, though thou hast not thy bliss,
For ever wilt thou love, and she be fair!

Ah, happy, happy boughs! that cannot shed
  Your leaves, nor ever bid the Spring adieu;
And happy melodist, unwearièd,
  For ever piping songs for ever new;
More happy love! more happy, happy love!
  For ever warm, and still to be enjoy'd,
    For ever panting and for ever young;
All breathing human passion far above,
  That leaves a heart high-sorrowful and cloy'd,
    A burning forehead, and a parching tongue.

Who are these coming to the sacrifice?
  To what green altar, O mysterious priest,
Lead'st thou that heifer lowing at the skies,
  And all her silken flanks with garlands drest?
What little town by river or seashore,
  Or mountain-built with peaceful citadel,
    Is emptied of this folk, this pious morn?
And, little town, thy streets for evermore
  Will silent be; and not a soul to tell
    Why thou art desolate, can e'er return.

O Attic shape! Fair attitude! with brede
  Of marble men and maidens overwrought,
With forest branches and the trodden weed;
  Thou, silent form, dost tease us out of thought
As doth eternity: Cold Pastoral!
  When old age shall this generation waste,
    Thou shalt remain, in midst of other woe
Than ours, a friend to man, to whom thou say'st,
"Beauty is truth, truth beauty,"—that is all
  Ye know on earth, and all ye need to know.

John Keats

THE HOME OF HELEN

Lacedæmon, hast thou seen it?
Lacedæmon, Lacedæmon!
Round Taygetus the forests
Leaguer snow-capped crags above them.
Lacedæmon, rich in corn-lands,
With the grand hill-shoulders round them
Blue as lapis in the twilight,
Striking early every morning
Through the mist till when the azure
Drops a veil of lucent sapphire
O'er our mountains in the noon-tide—
Our old ramparts, walls of safety!

And Eurotas—hast thou heard him,
Heard Eurotas, old Eurotas,
Gurgle, growl and gnaw the boulders?
Hast thou heard Eurotas laughing?
Hast thou stemmed his solemn current,
Where the dark rose-laurels shade it,
In the cool cliff-sheltered places,
Where the women bathe, while gravely
Swans sail in and out among them?
—Swimming women, in pure water
Passing 'neath swans proud and passive,
Where Zeus saw and loved white Leda?

                              T. Sturge Moore

THE PARTHENON BY MOONLIGHT

This is an island of the golden Past
   Uplifted in the tranquil sea of night.
In the white splendor how the heart beats fast,
   When climbs the pilgrim to this gleaming height;
As might a soul, new-born, its wondering way
   Take through the gates of pearl and up the stair
Into the precincts of celestial day,
   So to this shrine my worshiping feet did fare.

But look! what tragic waste! Is Time so lavish
   Of dear perfection thus to see it spilled?
'Twas worth an empire;—now behold the ravish
   That laid it low. The soaring plain is filled
With the wide-scattered letters of one word
   Of loveliness that nevermore was spoken;
Nor ever shall its like again be heard:
   Not dead is art—but that high charm is broken.

Now moonlight builds with swift and mystic art
   And makes the ruin whole—and yet not whole;
But exquisite, tho' crusht and torn apart.
   Back to the temple steals its living soul
In the star-silent night; it comes all pale—
   A spirit breathing beauty and delight,
And yet how stricken! Hark! I hear it wail
   Self-sorrowful, while every wound bleeds white.

And tho' more sad than is the nightingale
   That mourns in Lykabettos' fragrant pine,
That soul to mine brings solace; nor shall fail
   To heal the heart of man while still doth shine

Yon planet, doubly bright in this deep blue;
  Yon moon that brims with fire these violet hills.
For beauty is of God; and God is true,
  And with His strength the soul of mortal fills.

                              Richard Watson Gilder

NATIONAL AIR

GREECE

Ah, 'tis thou, I know the gleaming,
  Of thy sword so keen and bright
And I know that glance embracing,
  All the world within its light—
For thee, sprung from blood of heroes,
  Liberty, the tyrants quail.
Hail, oh, Freedom, Hail, oh, Freedom,
  Ours the Victory, all Hail,
Hail, oh, Freedom, Hail, oh, Freedom,
  Ours the Victory, all Hail.

N. Manzaros

Land of a glorious sunshine; noted for the mighty cathedral of Seville, for the departed Moor and for the Alhambra; a land which still lives in the glory of a great past, where the Spanish grandee is a living picture by Velasquez or El Greco; land whose peoples still dream of the Cid and the Conquistadores, of Don Quixote and of Sancho Panza, and of Isabella and the day when her mighty galleons sailed the seas and brought back the wealth of Eldorados for the courts of Spain; nation whose national sport is the bull fight; who lives still in the Middle Ages, waiting for western progress to waken her into new life.

ABENCERRAGE

Canto II, L. I.

Fair land; Of chivalry the old domain
Land of the vine and olive; Lovely Spain
Though not for thee with classic shores to vie
In charms that fix th' enthusiast's pensive eye
Yet hast thou scenes of beauty richly fraught
With all that wakes the glow of lofty thought.

Felicia D. Hemans

THE ROAD TO GRANADA

All day, the burning furnace of the plain;
   Bare mountains white with sun—the distances
Breathless, unbroken, save where olive trees
   Spent their scant shade and weary fields of grain
Ebbed in the heat like an enchanted main
   On the wrapt shores of some Hesperides.
Still little towns—as sun besieged as these,
   A hill-top tower glimpsed and lost again—
Who guessed this wonder at the journey's close?
   The shining towers, the leafy long Ravine,
Shadows and murmuring water everywhere!
   Above, Sierra with its crown of snow—
And, midway-set, in gardens, hung in air,
   Alhambra, throned and lovely like a queen!

Arthur Ketchum

THE GIRL OF CADIZ

Oh, never talk again to me
   Of northern climes and British ladies;
It has not been your lot to see,
Like me, the lovely Girl of Cadiz.
Although her eye be not of blue,
   Nor fair her locks, like English lasses,
How far its own expressive hue
   The languid azure eye surpasses!

Prometheus-like, from heaven she stole
   The fire, that through those silken lashes
In darkest glances seems to roll,
   From eyes that cannot hide their flashes;
And as along her bosom steal
   In lengthen'd flow her raven tresses,
You'd swear each clustering lock could feel,
   And curl'd to give her neck caresses.

Our English maids are long to woo,
   And frigid even in possession;
And if their charms be fair to view,
   Their lips are slow at Love's confession;
But, born beneath a brighter sun,
   For love ordain'd the Spanish maid is,
And who,—when fondly, fairly won,—
   Enchants you like the Girl of Cadiz?

The Spanish maid is no coquette,
   Nor joys to see a lover tremble;
And if she love, or if she hate,
   Alike she knows not to dissemble.

Her heart can ne'er be bought or sold,—
  Howe'er it beats, it beats sincerely;
And, though it will not bend to gold,
  'Twill love you long, and love you dearly.

The Spanish girl that meets your love
  Ne'er taunts you with a mock denial,
For every thought is bent to prove
  Her passion in the hour of trial.
When thronging foemen menace Spain
  She dares the deed and shares the danger;
And should her lover press the plain,
  She hurls the spear, her love's avenger.

And when, beneath the evening star,
  She mingles in the gay Bolero,
Or sings to her attuned guitar
  Of Christian knight or Moorish hero,
Or counts her beads with fairy hand
  Beneath the twinkling rays of Hesper,
Or joins Devotion's choral band
  To chaunt the sweet and hallowed vesper,—

In each her charms the heart must move
  Of all who venture to behold her;
Then let not maids less fair reprove
  Because her bosom is not colder:
Through many a clime 'tis mine to roam
  Where many a soft and melting maid is,
But none abroad, and few at home,
  May match the dark-eyed Girl of Cadiz.

Lord Byron

CASTLES IN SPAIN

How much of my young heart, O Spain,
　Went out to thee in days of yore!
What dreams romantic filled my brain,
And summoned back to life again
The Paladins of Charlemain,
　The Cid Campeador!

And shapes more shadowy than these,
　In the dim twilight half revealed;
Phœnician galleys on the seas,
The Roman camps like hives of bees,
The Goth uplifting from his knees
　Pelayo on his shield.

It was these memories perchance,
　From annals of remotest eld,
That lent the colors of romance
To every trivial circumstance
And changed the form and countenance
　Of all that I beheld.

Old towns, whose history lies hid
　In monkish chronicle or rhyme,—
Burgos, the birthplace of the Cid,
Zamora and Valladolid,
Toledo, built and walled amid
　The wars of Wamba's time;

The long, straight line of the highway,
　The distant town that seems so near,
The peasants in the fields, that stay
Their toil to cross themselves and pray,
When from the belfry at midday
　The Angelus they hear;

White crosses in the mountain pass,
　Mules gay with tassels, the loud din
Of muleteers, the tethered ass
That crops the dusty wayside grass,
And cavaliers with spurs of brass
　Alighting at the inn;

White hamlets hidden in fields of wheat,
　White cities slumbering by the sea,
White sunshine flooding square and street,
Dark mountain-ranges, at whose feet
The river-beds are dry with heat,—
　All was a dream to me.

Yet something sombre and severe
　O'er the enchanted landscape reigned;
A terror in the atmosphere
As if King Philip listened near,
Or Torquemada, the austere,
　His ghostly sway maintained.

The softer Andalusian skies
　Dispelled the sadness and the gloom;
There Cadiz by the seaside lies,
And Seville's orange-orchards rise,
Making the land a paradise
　Of beauty and of bloom.

There Cordova is hidden among
　The palm, the olive, and the vine;
Gem of the South, by poets sung,
And in whose Mosque Almanzor hung
As lamps the bells that once had rung
　At Compostella's shrine.

But over all the rest supreme,
    The star of stars, the cynosure,
The artist's and the poet's theme,
The young man's vision, the old man's dream,—
Granada by its winding stream,
    The city of the Moor!

And there the Alhambra still recalls
    Aladdin's palace of delight:
Allah il Allah! through its halls
Whispers the fountain as it falls,
The Darro darts beneath its walls,
    The hills with snow are white.

Ah, yes, the hills are white with snow,
    And cold with blasts that bite and freeze;
But in the happy vale below
The orange and pomegranate grow,
The wafts of air toss to and fro
    The blossoming almond-trees.

The Vega cleft by the Xenil,
    The fascination and allure
Of the sweet landscape chains the will;
The traveller lingers on the hill,
His parted lips are breathing still
    The last sigh of the Moor.

How like a ruin overgrown
    With flowers that hide the rents of time,
Stands now the Past that I have known;
Castles in Spain, not built of stone
But of white summer cloud, and blown
    Into this little mist of rhyme!

                        Henry Wadsworth Longfellow

NATIONAL AIR

Hail him! Hail him! All hail our noble king Alfonso,
Hail to our king, our noble King Alfonso,
Laurel encrowns him, and Love guides his hand
To rule with justice o'er this loyal land!

Hail him! Hail him! All hail our noble king Alfonso!

Traditional March

HOMEWARD BOUND

GIBRALTAR

Seven weeks of sea, and twice seven days of storm
Upon the huge Atlantic, and once more
We ride into still water and the calm
Of a sweet evening screened by either shore
Of Spain and Barbary. Our toils are o'er,
Our exile is accomplished. Once again
We look on Europe, mistress as of yore
Of the fair earth and of the hearts of men.
Ay, this is the famed rock, which Hercules
And Goth and Moor bequeathed us. At this door
England stands sentry. God! to hear the shrill
Sweet treble of her fifes upon the breeze
And at the summons of the rock gun's roar
To see her red coats marching from the hill.

Wilfrid Scawen Blunt

HOME-THOUGHTS FROM THE SEA

Nobly, nobly Cape Saint Vincent to the northwest died
  away;
Sunset ran, one glorious blood-red, reeking into Cadiz Bay;
Bluish mid the burning water, full in face Trafalgar lay;
In the dimmest northeast distance, dawned Gibraltar grand
  and gray;
"Here and here did England help me:—how can I help
  England?"—say,
Whoso turns as I, this evening, turn to God to praise and
  pray,
While Jove's planet rises yonder, silent over Africa.

Robert Browning

HILLS OF HOME

Name me no names for my disease,
  With uninforming breath;
I tell you I am none of these,
  But homesick unto death—

Homesick for hills that I have known,
  For brooks that I had crossed,
Before I met this flesh and bone
  And followed and was lost. . . .

And though they break my heart at last,
  Yet name no name of ills.
Say only, "Here is where he passed,
  Seeking again these hills."

                              Witter Bynner

INDEX

INDEX TO AUTHORS

INDEX TO FIRST LINES